TravelScan

merican Red Cross
.420, 47.520, 47.460,
.540, 47.50

Henry & Eric Eisenson

ederal Emergency Management Agency (FEMA)
8.575, 142.350, 139.450, 142.425, 139.950, 142.450

S DOE Nuclear Emergency Search Team (NEST)
9.220, 164.400, 150.450,164.475, 164.025, 164.525,
100, 164.675, 164.175, 164.700, 164.225, 164.775,
4.75

TravelScan

ational Transportation Safety Board
5.50   Channel 1
5.52   Channel 2
6.75   Channel 3

National Search and Rescue

40.500	US Military joint operations
47.460	National Jeep Search and Rescue
121.500	Civilian ELT
121.600	US/Canada On-Scene S&R
138.450	Air Rescue Service On-Scene
138.780	Air Rescue Service
156.300	Merchant ship/USGC Channel 6 On-Scene
156.800	Maritime Channel 16 Distress/Safety/Calling
156.750	Maritime Class C Channel 15 Calling
243.000	Military Aeronautical Emergency
259.000	Air Rescue
381.000	Air Rescue Operations
381.800	USCG Aircraft Working Frequency
406.500	ELT

Emergency, Recreation, and Government Frequencies Across America

Civil Air Patrol (CAP)

26.620	AM
121.500	Civilian AeronauticalEmergency/ELT/EPIRB
121.600	ELT Testing
122.900	SAR
123.100	SAR
143.900	SAR (AM/FM)

Paladin Press • Boulder, Colorado

Other books by Henry Eisenson:
Scanners and Secret Frequencies

TravelScan: Emergency, Recreation, and Government Frequencies Across America
by Henry and Eric Eisenson

Copyright © 1999 by Henry and Eric Eisenson

ISBN 1-58160-053-4
Printed in the United States of America

Published by Paladin Press, a division of
Paladin Enterprises, Inc., P.O. Box 1307,
Boulder, Colorado 80306, USA.
(303) 443-7250

Direct inquiries and/or orders to the above address.

PALADIN, PALADIN PRESS, and the "horse head" design
are trademarks belonging to Paladin Enterprises and
registered in United States Patent and Trademark Office.

Visit our Web site at www.paladin-press.com

Contents

Introduction
and Credits

This book was written for one reason: we couldn't buy it. It would have been a lot easier if we could have talked someone else into doing this job, but that just didn't happen.

We travel a lot, and have frequently prepared a list of frequencies for the stops on our scheduled itinerary. But when travel plans changed, we could either find a local source for new information, or try to scan for it. What we needed was a pocket guide that wouldn't take much space in a briefcase, and that would fuel the appetite of our scanner's memory. Just programming the huge memory of some of today's portable/mobile units takes long enough to keep the average hobbyist out of trouble.

This book was not designed to change your vacation plans, but if you're a scanner enthusiast it will make your trip more enjoyable. It was fun to write, because we had many interesting dialogs with hobbyists and experts across the country, whose insights regarding their hometowns went beyond just scanner frequencies. We learned about politics, road conditions, radio monitoring, and scanner clubs, the best places to get a drink, local stores, state law, military bases, local job conditions, and much more. Those phone calls were welcome and useful, and all those who helped build this book have earned our gratitude and that of the many other hobbyists who will find it useful.

We also owe thanks to all those who bought the first edition of this book (published by Index Publishing) and corrected our errors! This book is specifically dedicated to the center of the scanning industry . . . those few who have worked so hard to contribute so much, to so many, for so long, and have earned mostly applause. It must be a passion, because in any other industry the same brain-power and effort would make these people rich. For their guidance, insights, and fountains of critical scanner information, the authors specifically thank:

Linton Vandiver, Index's publisher, who raised the mark in the scanner hobby publishing business by introducing a new perspective and demanding a new level of quality. He brought to this market more than 35 years of experience in professional and medical publishing, and demanded the utmost in performance from his writers.

Bill Cheek, publisher of the *World Scanner Report* and author of *The Ultimate Scanner.* Don't miss his monthly column in *Monitoring Times*, which drips with the "hot scoop" and is one of the most impressive forums of scanner lore in the hobby today. All three people who understand his math agree that Bill is the most technically competent writer in the field.

Norm Schrein, author of *Emergency Radio!* He's "Mr. Scanner" to the thousands of members of the Bearcat Radio Club, and knows as much about enjoying a scanner as Cheek does about modifying them.

Thomas J. Arey wrote *Radio Monitoring: The How-To Guide*, in which reposes an enormous store of information about radio monitoring from DC to daylight. This is probably the scanning hobby's most authoritative and comprehensive book.

Thomas Kneitel, author of almost everything else, has compiled more information about scanning than anyone else we know.

Thanks to these gurus!

Using This Book

NO LOGIC

There was no perfect way to organize this book; we knew it would be impossible to please everyone. After talking with many hobbyists about what they'd like to see, how they'd like to work with the information presented here, we found general disagreement. So we pleased ourselves, and the result is the Table of Contents.

The national section includes a lot of general data, including frequency allocations, military usage, and national licenses issued by the FCC to interesting licensees.

The states are listed alphabetically. There are 51 listings including the District of Columbia. Cities are listed alphabetically under the state in which they're located. Entries include a few comments that go beyond the scanner hobby, but some of them might be entertaining or useful.

We strongly recommend a visit to the Internet before you leave on your trip. We've provided some sources for the latest frequency information, and most of those sources are "linked" to others. Take advantage of this exciting resource!

STAY ALIVE AT 65

Our publisher asked, "Why are those speed traps in there?" We figured that if you were busy listening to your scanner (our fault because this book made it so much fun to do that), you might miss that speed limit sign behind the carefully trimmed tree. It made sense to try to level the playing field by giving you an advance warning. We've listed a few places where it makes great sense to pay attention to the speedometer rather than to the scanner.

FREQUENCIES

Throughout this book, unless specified otherwise, all frequency references are in megahertz (MHz).

For most cities we listed only a few frequencies, but tried to focus upon those which should be the most active and/or the most useful. To find more frequencies, begin with what we've given you and *scan*. As an example, if we list 461.125, 461.225, and 154.6 MHz for a certain city, that will tell you where to scan for more. You can use your scanner to find new frequencies in each city you visit, but start with the frequencies we provide because they indicate the bands in which that city's system operates. For most cities we provided only the basic frequencies for police dispatcher, fire, and emergency medical—under the heading "Emergency Services."

Trunking provides great spectrum efficiency to the communication system, but is a challenge to the hobbyist. If you have a scanner that automatically follows trunking, great! Most scanners are baffled by such frequency-hopping and require that you enter the trunking system's frequency range and step size (channel separation), and even then you'll hear things in a rather disjointed way. In those areas where trunking dominates, we have provided that frequency range. We suggest that you scan within that range using the finest steps you can, and keep notes (pull over for this!). When you have determined the frequency steps of a particular trunking system you can program your scanner accordingly. When available, we have added some conventional frequencies.

ERRORS

There are *NO ERRORS IN THIS BOOK! NONE!* If you discover something that seems incorrect, it was deliberately included to test your perception, comprehension, and understanding of the hobby. When you can suggest an improvement, send the publisher a comprehensive letter and after he evaluates your writing skills perhaps you'll get a book contract.

There is no index. Use the Table of Contents—and common sense. If it's not here but you wish it were, send the publisher a note.

And if you *must* read while driving, look up once in a while.

the relay frequencies used between the portable radios carried by police and highway patrol officers and the vehicles they operate. That gives the user an alert when such a police radio is within about a half mile. Such receivers are generally not very flexible; in addition to that very special function, they are usually configured to include state-by-state preprogramming and do not allow the user to program non-law-enforcement frequencies of interest.

Handheld scanners operate from internal batteries, though most permit the use of an external source such as the proper cable to a car's cigarette lighter. They range from elementary 10-channel pre-programmed designs (and if you have one of these, why are you reading this?) to some of the most sophisticated radio products available to a civilian.

HOW ABOUT ANTENNAS?

Well, virtually all significant programmable scanners support an external antenna. A reasonably correct mobile antenna can be magnetically or mechanically attached to the car, and connected to the scanner using an industry-standard BNC connector. "Reasonably correct?" That's because every antenna is ideal for *one* specific frequency or its multiple, and at other frequencies it is less than ideal.

If you wish to monitor a specific portion of the frequency spectrum, then with any given antenna all but one or two frequencies will involve a compromise. But unless you're a perfectionist, or trying to listen to some specific station that's really weak and/or distant from your location, almost *any* antenna will be at least OK if it's located properly.

In another book (*Scanners & Secret Frequencies*) one of this book's authors claimed that only a very few people truly understand antennas. That statement produced criticism by people who said they have generated good mathematical models of antenna function, have built/designed antennas of various sorts, and otherwise demonstrated their antenna-competence. Well, after extensive dialog with these well-meaning folks, and with one of the half-dozen or so truly competent antenna theorists in the field, we'll stick to the original statement and embellish it as follows: being able to follow instructions to produce an antenna of the proper length, and with the proper directors and reflectors, all of the appropriate configuration and impedances, does *not* mean that the antenna is "understood." Does the cook understand what happens to the egg protein molecules when he scrambles it? Does he need to?

Don't worry about the length of the antenna, as anything you pick will probably be close enough because it will come close to one of the important lengths for almost any frequency you select (5/8-l, half-l, quarter-l, full-l or whatever). It will be right for some frequencies and wrong for others, but close enough . . . By the way, l (lambda) means "wavelength," or the speed of light divided by the frequency of the signal, so obviously every frequency has a different wavelength. Effectiveness of an antenna depends primarily upon its length with respect to the wavelength of a given signal.

If you want things to get really complicated, this is where to begin. If you prefer listening to your scanner rather than spending time on a Cray Supercomputer, anything that's a foot or two in length will probably work fine, as the primary objective of the external antenna and cable is to move that critical function out of that metal vehicle (an insulator) and into the aether, where it belongs.

If you really wish improve your antenna, perhaps for a specific signal that's worth the effort, keep the math simple. The l of a 300 MHz signal is about a meter. At twice the frequency, l becomes half; at twice that, it's half again, and so forth. At 900 MHz (the cellular range, as an example), you're working at three times that 300 MHz memory helper, hence l is 1/3 of that meter, or about 33 cm. That's more or less 13~. Therefore, for a 900 MHz signal:

Full wave	13~
5/8 wave	8~
Half wave	6.5~
Quarter wave	3.25~

Since a half-l antenna works pretty well (and you don't want to pay for "works perfectly"), six and a half inches is all anyone should ask for. If, on the other hand, you want to listen to civilian aviation communication a bit below 150 MHz, l is *two* meters; you figure it out . . . Don't make the antenna a big deal, but always use an *external* antenna when scanning from a vehicle.

CABLE

Most antennas are packaged with a cable that terminates in a BNC connector (a twist-on bayonet-style coaxial connector) suitable for the "external antenna" jack on your scanner. To find that jack, and to identify any idiosyncrasies of your particular scanner, read the manual. Most handheld scanners use an antenna ("rubber duck") with a BNC base, so you'll never find a separate jack; just remove the antenna and attach the cable to the BNC connector.

When you run the cable from a magnetically-attached rooftop or lip-of-the-trunk clamp-on antenna into the passenger compartment, there's a temptation to let it simply go through the door or trunk opening. The assumption is that the rubber molding around the opening will cushion the cable and prevent damage. The threat, however, comes not from the grommet area but from the outer "lip," which can be quite sharp. If the cable slips to a point where the gap between the door and the body is narrow enough, the cable can be damaged. We recommend finding the best (widest) point, and then duct-taping the cable in place so it cannot shift to a narrower area. Try to do that taping inside — not outside — because a few days of sun can make some duct tape adhesives "cure" and adhere very tightly to the paint.

Keep the cable as short as practical, as there's significant loss per foot. That means you shouldn't use an antenna's original 25 foot cable, winding it into a coil under your seat. Rather, make a neat installation, and then cut the cable at the proper point and install a new BNC connector. It's an annoying task, but yes, it's worth it.

AUDIO

There will come a time when your scanner's little speaker is simply inadequate—particularly if your car, like mine, generates fairly loud wind noise at speeds over 120 mph. There are several solutions. Virtually all scanners today have earphone jacks, the output level of which is controllable by the volume control. Usually, a common "mini" coaxial plug is all that's needed to tap this source.

You might consider using earphones, but that's dangerous and in some jurisdictions it's illegal, because it limits your ability to respond to noise from outside the car. It also, however, reduces the need to respond to questions and driving suggestions from inside the car. *That* is often a terrific benefit that may even be worth an occasional ticket.

Radio Shack and other retailers of electronic gadgetry offer derivatives of an interesting gadget. It's a dummy cassette that goes into the conventional tape slot on the front of your stereo, but there's no magnetic tape inside. Instead, in the cassette housing there's a tape head positioned so it will match up with the tape head of the stereo, and the audio output from the scanner is fed directly to that tape head. Energy transfer is sufficient for good performance, but again, everyone in the vehicle must listen to the scanner. Such devices require pre-equalization because of the output curve of tape, but this often works satisfactorily. With this solution the tape player's motors are made to spin constantly, and that will annoy those who always place their drinks in the precise center of the coaster. You know who you are.

Many of today's car radio/tape players have "auxiliary" or "CD" input jacks on the rear or front panel, plus a switch that allows selection of that input. Depending upon how difficult it is to reach the back of your radio, this might be a good solution. It means, however, that your traveling companion(s) must listen to the scanner—no choice.

Here's a favorite solution from the senior author, especially considering: (1) the state of my hearing and (2) my wife's taste for music on the car stereo. Get a small self-amplified speaker for $15 or so at Radio Shack, etc., and mount it on the visor, mirror, or door frame, pointed at your best ear (or use two in parallel). Connect that unit to your scanner with conventional audio shielded cable.

Assuming the amplifier is equipped with a power input, get an adapter (another $10) for your cigarette lighter and make certain that both voltage and polarity are correct. Dress the wires carefully behind the window molding, and you're in business. To avoid marital strife, use the stereo's balance control to shift the car's audio to the *right* channel (if you're driving a 1934 Rolls Royce Silver Ghost, the passenger sits on the LEFT, so reverse those instructions); that will let your wife listen as she chooses without too much conflict with the stations you're monitoring.

Try to find an amplified speaker with tone controls. If you cannot find one and you (like me) need a bit more treble, you may wish to boost the high end with a variable resistor and capacitor in series. For most little amplified speakers, the input impedance is such that a 10k ohm potentiometer and a 0.001 mfd capacitor will give the desired treble boost. Experiment:

In the drawing, when the potentiometer is at "max" resistance (the arrow to the right), more of the signal must pass through the capacitor. Since capacitors pass higher frequencies more readily than low frequencies, more treble will be amplified. In effect, this simple circuit is an adjustable treble control.

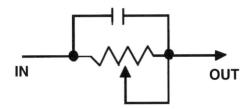

When pursuing this option, there are certain minor hazards. Unless you carefully check polarity and voltage from the adapter and match them properly, you may need at least two of the speakers. A mistake will definitely cost a few bucks.

GOOD COMBINATIONS

This book assumes that you travel, have a programmable scanner that runs either from vehicle or battery power, have a reasonably competent external antenna, that the two are properly cabled together, and that you haven't memorized the entire FCC frequency allocation.

Refer to *Recommended Reading for Boring Motel Evenings* if you need help deciding which hardware is most suited to your requirement, or is modifiable to meet your tastes. That's where you'll also find a wealth of available frequency lists that far surpass this pocket guide quick reference.

Success on the road takes good hardware, the required frequencies, and a reasonable strategy. That's next.

Programming
Strategies

Do your programming when stopped for the night, pulled over to the side, at a restaurant, or in the rest room, but *NEVER WHILE DRIVING*. We'd like you to be around to buy the next edition of this book.

Programmable scanners usually group their available "addresses" (frequencies) into banks. For instance, a 100-frequency scanner might offer 10 banks, each with 10 available locations in which frequencies can be programmed. The hobbyist might put the police tactical frequencies in one bank, fire and other emergency services into another, military into a third, and so forth. Or, he/she might lump all transmitters from one general area (the southeast part of the city, as an example) into one bank.

Everyone has his own style, which usually evolves based upon available equipment (how many banks, with how many frequencies each), and the interest of the listener. When we use a scanner in our hometown, we quickly gravitate to some programming strategy that fits well with what's happening, where, and our specific interests and inclinations. Those "home" strategies, unfortunately, are rarely correct for the road. When traveling, you lose some of the factors that defined your programming strategy at home. So let's assume that you're on the road. What's the best approach?

Let's assume that you have not yet implemented mods from Jerry Pickard (*Scanner Modifications and Antennas*) and/or Bill Cheek (*The Ultimate Scanner*), so instead of 153.6676 gazillion frequencies you "only" have 200 channels available, organized as 10 banks of 20 frequencies each.

Suppose you're planning to pass through three major cities the next day of travel. Here's one way you might set up the memory the night before.

Bank	Frequencies
1	City 1 police and sheriff
2	City 1 fire and emergency services
3	City 2 police and sheriff
4	City 2 fire and emergency services
5	City 3 police and sheriff
6	City 3 fire and emergency services

The first six banks are set up for the cities through which you plan to travel. The next four banks are set up as follows:

Bank	Frequencies
7	State/county highway patrol and services
8	National 3-letter agencies, including park and forestry services
9	Commercial and general aviation
10	Military and special interests

Suppose you're passing through a remote area and want news regarding local conditions, etc. Program the park or ranger frequencies into Bank 10. Thanks to the published modifications of Cheek and Pickard, we can have more banks than Chase Manhattan, but if your scanner isn't yet modified, part of Bank 10 might be used for anything that's temporary and of special interest during some part of the trip.

If your scanner covers the citizens band (CB), even if you're short of channels you should set aside a few of them for Trucker Common and emergency transmissions.

Generally, your overall programming objectives are to. . .

- find what you're looking for without taking too much attention from your driving.
- establish a pattern that makes it quick and logical to do your "night before" programming.
- set up an arrangement that matches your specific interests with available communication in the area through which you're traveling.

And as you page through this book, remember: all frequencies are in megahertz unless specified otherwise.

Frequencies that Work Everywhere

EVERYWHERE?

Well, that is a *very* impressive chapter title, but it's our first lie. Nothing is forever, and no frequency works everywhere. This chapter, however, lists many frequencies on which you *should* hear interesting radio traffic across *most* of these United States.

GENERAL FREQUENCY ALLOCATIONS

This listing is more useful than it might initially appear. Not only does it provide allocations of specific frequency bands to users, it also provides either direct information or clues to channel separation (steps) and modulation of typical signals in many of the described bands. The channel step information is especially useful when trying to scan bands that are trunked.

MHz	Usage
30-50	FM, 20 kHz steps
30-30.56	U.S. government
30.56-31.98	Business/industry/forestry
31.99-32	Public safety

32-33	U.S. government
33-33.1	Public safety
33.12-33.4	Business/petroleum
33.42-34	Fire
34-35	U.S. government
35.02-36	Business/paging
36-37	U.S. government
37.02-37.42	Police/local government
37.46-37.86	Power/water/pipeline
37.9-38	Highway maintenance/spec emerg
38-39	U.S. government
39.02-40	Police/local government
40-42	U.S. government
42.02-42.94	State police/highway patrol
42.96-43.68	Business/paging
43.7-43.6	Transportation/bus/truck
44.62-45.06	State police/forestry
45.08-45.86	Police/local government/highway
45.9-46.04	Police/emergency
46.06-46.5	Fire
46.52-46.58	Local government
46.61-46.97	Cordless phones (base)
47.02-47.4	Highway maintenance
47.44-47.68	Industry/emergency
47.7-49.58	Industry
49.67-49.99	Cordless phones (handset)
50-54	Ham, 6 meter band
54-72	Broadcast TV, Ch 2-4, wideband FM
72-76	Unspecified (extraterrestrial telepathy)
76-88	Broadcast TV, Ch 5-6, wideband FM
88.1-107.9	FM commercial broadcast
108-118	Aviation navigation
118-136	Comm'l air, 25 kHz steps, AM
136-138	Satellite
138-144	U.S. government
144-148	Ham, 2 meter band
148-150.8	U.S. government

150.815-150.965	Auto emergency
150.995-151.595	Highway/forestry/industry
151.625-151.955	Business, 30 kHz steps
152.03-152.24	Mobile phone (base), page
152.27-152.45	Taxi (base)
152.51-152.84	Mobile phone (base), page
152.87-153.725	Industry
153.74-154.445	Fire/government mobile
154.49-154.625	Industry
154.65-156.24	Police/gov't/emergency highway
156.025-157.425	Maritime, 25 kHz steps
157.47-157.515	Auto emergency
157.53-157.71	Taxi (mobile)/business
157.77-158.1	Mobile phone (mobile)
158.13-158.46	Industry
158.49-158.7	Mobile phone (mobile)
158.73-159.21	Police/government/highway
159.225-159.465	Forestry
159.495-160.2	Transportation, bus/truck
160.215-161.61	Railroad
160.625-160.95	Maritime, 25 kHz steps
161.64-161.76	Broadcast pickups
161.5-162.025	Maritime, 25 kHz
162.025-174	U.S. government
174-216	B'cast TV, Ch 7-13, wideband FM
216-218	Maritime AMTS coast, 25 kHz
218-219	Interactive video and data
219-220	Maritime AMTS ship, 25 kHz
220.0025-220.9975	General (trunked) base, 5 kHz
221.0025-221.9975	General (trunked) mobile, 5 kHz
222-225	Ham, 1.25 meter band
225-400	Mil aviation, 25 kHz steps, AM
400-406	U.S. gov't meteorological, space
406-420	U.S. government
420-450	Ham, mil radar, direction finding
450-455	FM base, 25 kHz steps
455-460	FM mobile, 25 kHz steps

450.05-450.925	Broadcast aux
451.025-452.025	Industry
452.05-452.5	Taxi/industry/transport
452.525-452.6	Auto emergency
452.625-452.95	Transportation/trucks/railroad
452.975-453	Relay press
453.025-453.975	Local government, public safety
454.025-454.65	Mobile telephone
454.675-454.975	Mobile telephone air/ground
455.05-455.925	Broadcast aux
456.025-457.025	Industry
457.05-457.5	Taxi/industry/transport
457.525-457.6	Maritime ship repeater/bus lo-pwr
457.625-457.95	Transportation/trucks
457.975-458	Relay press
458.025-458.975	Local gov't/public safety
459.025-459.65	Mobile telephone
459.675-459.975	Mobile telephone (air)
460-465	FM, 25 kHz steps, base
465-470	FM, 25 kHz steps, mobile
460.025-460.55	Police, public safety
460.575-460.625	Fire
460.65-460.875	Business/airport
460.9-461	Business/alarms
461.025-462.175	Business
462.2-462.525	Mfg/industry
462.55-462.725	GMRS, 12.5 kHz steps
462.75-462.925	Business paging
462.95-463.175	Ambulance/hospital/medical
463.2-465	Business
465.025-465.55	Police, public safety
465.575-465.625	Fire
465.65-465.875	Business/airport
465.9-466	Business/alarms
466.025-467.175	Business
467.2-467.525	Mfg/industry
467.55-467.725	GMRS, 25 kHz steps

467.75-467.825	Maritime shipboard
467.75-457.925	Business, 2-way telemetry
467.95-468.175	Ambulance/hospital
468.2-469.975	Business
470-806	Broadcast TV
806-851	FM, 25 kHz, mobile
851-896	FM, 25 kHz, base
806.0125-809.7375	General-conventional/trunked
854.7625-855.9875	General-single channels
856.0125-860.9875	Conventional trunking band
861.0125-865.9875	SMR trunked
866.0125-868.9875	Pub safety, trunked, 12.5 kHz steps
869.04-879.36	Cellular phones, 30 kHz steps
879.39-880.62	Cellular phones, data, 30 kHz steps
880.65-893.97	Cellular phones, 30 kHz steps
894.0055-895.9735	A/C telephone, 6 kHz steps
896-901	SMR/mobile, 12.5 kHz steps
901-902	Personal comm
902-928	Ham, 33 cm band
928-929	Unspecified (Roswell UFO comm)
929-930	Paging
930-931	Personal comm svc, base
931-935	Unspecified (UFO intership comm)
935-940	SMR/business, base, 12.5 kHz steps
940-941	Personal comm, base
941-960	Unspecified (Area 51 forcefield)
960-1215	Aviation navigation
1215-1240	U.S. government radio location/space
1240-1300	Ham, 23 cm band

Do not be surprised to discover operation in many bands which do not correspond with this general guide. The FCC has the authority to grant licenses for usages that do not comply with this table. Usually, such deviations occur based upon geography. If there is no licensee for some frequency or frequency band in the applicant's area, the FCC may grant a license (usually temporary but possibly permanent) to an applicant with requirements that cannot be met by the band in which that applicant's business or operation ordinarily communicates.

Certain government agencies have been known to operate in non-government bands, usually with an odd channel spacing or modulation. That is, the government might use amplitude modulation in 20 kHz steps that begin with XXX.225 MHz in a band where licensed users operate at *frequency* modulation at XXX.22, XXX.23, XXX.24, etc. At most, licensed users might hear a bit of noise.

If your scanner can tune in frequency steps as fine as 1 kHz, and you scan long enough in "unspecified" bands, you might discover narrowband signals that will surprise you. But when you're traveling, you usually cannot take time to "scan." You want to know who's working on what frequency, and program your receiver accordingly. The table we've provided is *not* classified or restricted as it would be by virtually every other country in the world, but is given by the FCC to anyone who asks, and is published at various levels of detail by many companies. The most comprehensive of those resources list virtually *all* licensees, nationwide, on CDROM.

EMERGENCY

Nationwide Interagency Frequencies

150.775	Emergency Portables
150.790	Emergency Portables
153.830	Fire/Fireground
154.265	Fire Mutual Aid
154.280	Fire Mutual Aid
154.295	Fire Mutual Aid
155.175	Emergency Medical Services
155.475	National Law Enforcement
155.205	Emergency Medical Services
155.235	Emergency Medical Services
866.0125	National Public Safety Calling
866.5125	National Public Safety Mutual Aid/Tactical
867.0125	National Public Safety Mutual Aid/Tactical
867.5125	National Public Safety Mutual Aid/Tactical
868.0125	National Public Safety Mutual Aid/Tactical

National Search and Rescue Frequencies
40.500   US Military joint operations
47.460   National Jeep Search and Rescue
121.500   Civilian ELT/EPIRB
121.600   US/Canada On-Scene S&R
138.450   Air Rescue Service On-Scene
138.780   Air Rescue Service On-Scene (discrete)
156.300   Merchant ship/USGC Channel 6 On-Scene
156.800   Maritime Channel 16 (Distress/Safety/Calling)
156.750   Maritime Class C EPIRB 15-second homing sig
243.000   Military Aeronautical Emergency
259.000   Air Rescue Operations
381.000   Air Rescue Operations
381.800   USCG Aircraft Working Frequency
406.500   ELT

Civil Air Patrol (CAP)
26.620   AM
121.500   Civilian AeronauticalEmergency/ELT/EPIRB
121.600   ELT Testing
122.900   SAR
123.100   SAR
143.900   SAR (AM/FM)
148.125   Secondary
148.150   Primary
149.925   Packet Data
282.800   SAR DF/On-Scene Primary

American Red Cross
47.420, 47.520, 47.460, 47.540, 47.50

Federal Emergency Management Agency (FEMA)
138.575, 142.350, 139.450, 142.425, 139.950, 142.450

US DOE Nuclear Emergency Search Team (NEST)
149.220, 164.400, 150.450,164.475, 164.025, 164.525, 164.100, 164.675, 164.175, 164.700, 164.225, 164.775, 164.375

National Transportation Safety Board

165.750   Channel 1
165.7625   Channel 2
166.175   Channel 3

Hospital Paramedics

463.000	468.000	MED-1
463.025	468.025	MED-2
463.050	468.050	MED-3
463.075	468.075	MED-4
463.100	468.100	MED-5
463.125	468.125	MED-6
463.150	468.150	MED-7
463.175	468.175	MED-8
462.950	467.950	MED-9 (dispatch)
462.975	467.975	MED-10 (alternate dispatch)

MILITARY

This pastime is pretty boring unless your hobby is tracking military units, but if you're turned on by cries of "Post Seven all secure, *SIR!!*" here are some frequencies used nationally by our boys in uniform. Of course, the listening opportunities vary considerably from base to base. Where the infantry works out, you might hear, "When's the helo coming with the beer?" From a supply base you might hear, "OK, the guard went to the latrine. Grab the stuff and load up the truck!"

Military aviation is another matter entirely. Near an air training area you might hear, "Turtle One, this is Turtle Three. Let's drop down to 10,000 feet (*where oxygen masks can be safely removed*) and have a smoke, and then we'll burn a few thousand dollars worth of taxpayers' fuel getting back up here."

As some readers know, one of the authors of this book, Henry Eisenson, spent 22 years flying for the Marines (hours of boredom, moments of terror!). If military aviation fascinates you, set up "UHF GUARD" (243.0) as your priority channel. There's rarely a guard transmission, but those few are interesting and exciting (moments of terror). Then pick from the following.

Military air uses the range from 225 to 400 MHz, in 25 kHz steps, AM. Fixed-wing attack aircraft talk to ground controllers on UHF in that band, but ground-to-ground and ground-to-helo tactical is FM, in the 40 MHz range.

Nationwide military aviation frequencies include:

Naval air station towers	340.2, 360.2
Army air base towers	241.0
Most towers	257.8, 236.6
MAC command posts	319.4
SAC command Posts	311.0, 321.0
Tactical Air Command posts	381.3
Search & Rescue (SAR)	40.5
Air Force Command Post alert	413.45
Air Force One phone link	407.85, 415.7
	171.2875

AIR SHOW FREQUENCIES

Golden Knights (USA parachute team)	123.4, 32.3
Thunderbirds (USAF)	120.45, 294.7, 241.4, 273.5, 322.3, 382.9
Blue Angels (USN)	241.4, 250.8, 251.6, 384.4, 156.675, 156.725

COMMERCIAL AND PRIVATE AVIATION FACILITIES

"Hello Center, this is Delta 1211 Heavy, on Victor 34, 22 miles north of Oxbow Intersection at 35,000. We're encountering moderate turbulence. Can you get us a better altitude?"

Of course, if you're driving through beautiful downtown Oxbow watching a vicious thunderstorm out the window, you don't need your scanner to find out what the weather's like out there.

But some scannists do find it fascinating to listen to aviation communication. It's divided into two parts: commercial and "general." The latter applies to everything on which passengers pay no fare.

Here's a simple breakdown of the mass of radio transmissions involving aircraft:

Center (ARTCC)	Air Route Traffic Control Center, which plans, monitors, and controls flights passing through each area of authority. Each center passes transient aircraft to the next center, or to another control agency, as the flight progresses out of its area.
Tower	At each airport, the control tower handles aircraft not under positive control by the ARTCC or similar agency.
Ground Control	At each airport, ground control manages taxiing aircraft and ensures safety of ground operations.
Departure Control	Aircraft taking off are often passed to this agency, which manages departing traffic in dense control areas around airports.
Approach Control	Arriving aircraft are passed to this agency by the enroute controller. Approach control might guide the aircraft via electronic landmarks, or pass it to a GCA facility.
Ground Controlled Approach	GCA does radar control of landing aircraft. Ordinarily, such control is required when weather conditions are very poor.
Guard	121.5 and 243.0 MHz, monitored by ALL towers, centers, most aircraft, and by most hobbyists. These are the emergency channels, and their use is reserved for actual emergency transmissions.

COMMON AVIATION FREQUENCIES

Purpose	Frequency or band
Civil Air Patrol	148.15 (pri), 149.925, 26.625, 122.9, 123.1, 123.45, 123.475
Airline Company Frequencies	129.0 through 132.0
Airline Ground Frequencies	460.65 through 460.875
Air to Air	122.85, 122.9, 122.925, 123.1
National Flight Watch	122.0
Emergency/guard: commercial	121.5
Emergency/guard: military	243.0

COMMERCIAL AIRCRAFT TELEPHONE (AIR TO GROUND)

454.675, 454.950, 454.9, 454.85, 454.8, 454.75, 454.70, 454.725, 454.775, 454.825, 454.875, 454.925, 454.975

AIR ROUTE TRAFFIC CONTROL CENTERS (ARTCC)

This brief list shows only one or two frequencies for each center, which in reality is divided into many areas of responsibility. Listen on the given frequencies and take notes of "handoff" frequencies as aircraft fly from one sector to the next. In that manner, for each center you can quickly build a list of frequencies in use and the areas they cover.

To avoid confusion, remember that *all* sectors within the cognizance of a given center respond with the name of that center. For instance, Denver Center controls the air over Cheyenne, Wyoming. Aircraft reporting over Cheyenne talk to "Denver Center." Areas of responsibility have nothing to do with state lines, and each center controls aircraft over a very broad interstate area.

Albuquerque	132.8, 134.6
Atlanta	135.0
Boston	134.95, 134.4
Chicago	127.8, 125.2

Cleveland	126.75, 127.7
Denver	125.9, 134.7
Fort Worth	128.2, 133.1
Houston	134.35, 125.0
Indianapolis	135.25, 119.55
Jacksonville	134.85, 132.5
Kansas City	135.3, 127.35
Los Angeles	132.5, 128.6
Miami	134.6, 133.2
Memphis	119.3, 120.85
Minneapolis	125.5, 120.3
New York	133.7, 134.8
Oakland	126.9, 128.8
Salt Lake City	132.25, 133.4
San Juan	135.7, 118.15
Seattle	123.95, 121.4
Washington	133.85, 121.0

HIGH ALTITUDE ENROUTE FLIGHT ADVISORY SERVICE

Each center also operates a "high altitude" advisory service, applicable generally to aircraft above 20,000 feet.

Center	Frequency
Albuquerque	127.625, 134.825
Atlanta	135.475
Boston	133.925
Cleveland	135.425
Denver	124.675
Fort Worth	133.775
Houston	126.625
Indianapolis	134.825
Jacksonville	135.175
Kansas City	128.475
Los Angeles	135.9
Miami	132.725
Memphis	133.675

Minneapolis	135.675
New York	134.725
Oakland	135.7
Salt Lake City	133.025
Seattle	135.925
Washington	134.525

REMOTE AIR OPERATIONS

These frequencies have been set aside for operational communication in areas so remote that line-of-sight to ground facilities is not always possible from cruise altitudes.

The hobbyist won't need this information when driving, but from a cruise ship it's a good semi-reclining pastime after you finish your fourth unlimited buffet of the afternoon!

Area	Frequency
North Atlantic	131.8
Caribbean	130.55
Pacific	128.95

MARINE RADIO

Usage	Frequency
Intership Safety (low power)	156.3
Commercial	156.35, 156.4, 156.5, 156.5, 156.55, 156.55, 156.9, 156.95, 156.375, 156.875 156.975, 157.025, 157.425
Port Operations	156.6, 156.7, 161.6, 157.0, 156.275, 156.325, 156.675, 156.725
Distress/Emergency	156.8
U.S. Coast Guard	157.05, 157.075, 157.125, 157.175
Great Lakes, inland waterways, major rivers, canals	216.0125-217.9875 218.0125-219.9875 (in 25 kHz steps)

RADIO AND TELEVISION
"TACTICAL" COMMUNICATIONS

Some entertainment media companies acquire local licenses in various parts of the country. Others have national licenses, a few of which are listed below. In any case, perhaps the most dedicated listeners to these frequencies are the newshounds of the competing networks.

Network	Frequencies
ABC	450.8, 450.825, 450.1125, 450.9875, 455.9875, 450.675, 450.725, 450.8, 450.875, 450.675, 450.725, 450.775,
CBS	450.050, 450.0875, 450.5125, 450.150, 450.1875, 450.4125, 450.850, 450.8, 450.75, 450.7, 450.65, 450.6125, 450.5875, 450.4875, 450.45, 450.3875, 450.350, 450.3125, 450.2875, 450.250, 450.2125, 450.1125
CNN	452.975, 452.9625, 452.9875, 453.0
ESPN	464.5, 464.55, 464.6, 464.75, 469.5
General media	161.64, 161.67, 161.70, 161.73, 161.76, 450-451, 455-456

HAM REPEATERS, NATIONWIDE

29.62-29.68, 53.01-53.99, 145.1-145.5, 146.61-147.39, 223.94-224.98, 442.0-450.0, 919.0-922.0, 1282.0-1288.0

CITIZENS BAND (CB) RADIO—USE AM

CB is really an excellent way to keep up with the local traveler news, such as traffic jams up ahead and identifying great places to park highway patrol cars. It's also a great way to find good restaurants or motels. See the Speed Traps section of this book for amplifying information on ways the vacationer can use CB.

Emergency frequency is 9, truck frequencies are 11 and 19.

1	26.965	15	27.135	29	27.295
2	26.975	16	27.155	30	27.305
3	26.985	17	27.165	31	27.315
4	27.005	18	27.175	32	27.325
5	27.015	19	27.185	33	27.335
6	27.025	20	27.205	34	27.345
7	27.035	21	27.215	35	27.355
8	27.055	22	27.225	36	27.365
9	27.065	23	27.255	37	27.375
10	27.075	24	27.235	38	27.385
11	27.085	25	27.245	39	27.395
12	27.105	26	27.265	40	27.405
13	27.115	27	27.275		
14	27.125	28	27.285		

WEATHER FREQUENCIES
NATIONWIDE, 24 HOURS A DAY

162.55, 162.4, 162.475, 162.425, 162.45, 162.5, 162.525

PRESIDENTIAL FREQUENCIES

Most of these functions (and the frequencies they use) follow the president around from one location and event to another, and are not used only in Washington.

Usage	Frequency
White House Marine Guard	169.925
White House Landing Pad Control	164.1
White House Mobile Command	166.5125
White House Staff	167.825, 168.7875, 167.2875
Presidential Helicopter	34.95, 46.7, 46.75, 46.8, 122.85, 142.75, 265.80, 268.0, 361.6, 375.0
Air Force One Phone Link	407.850, 415.7, 162.6875
Treasury Security	407.750, 407.925

Law Enforcement	164.65
Limousines	165.0875, 166.2125, 164.8875
Dignitary Protection	414.775
Local Agency Coordination	155.475
Secret Service and Treasury	32.23, 165.7875
Uniform Units	414.675 (pri), 415.675, 414.95
Primary Operations	165.7875

VARIOUS OTHER GOVERNMENT AGENCIES

The biggest user of spectrum (other than entertainment) is the U.S. government. It would take a book—and good ones are available—to comprehensively discuss frequency allocations to government agencies, but here is a "short list" that is valid in all or most of the country.

Agency	Frequencies
AGRI	164.825
BATF	166.4625 (pri), 165.2875, 165.9125, 173.8875, 168.0, 414.7, 418.225, 418.25
INS	162.9, 163.625, 163.65, 163.675, 163.7, 163.725, 163.75, 163.775, 165.2375, 165.875, 168.975
Customs	165.2375, 166.4625, 166.5875
DEA	418.625 (pri), 418.75, 418.675, 418.950, 418.825, 418.9
Dept of Energy	164.325, 164.375
EPA	164.450, 164.5, 164.4125
FCC	167.050
Fed Prisons	170.650, 170.825, 170.875, 170.925
Fed Banks	415.1
FEMA	138.575
GSA Security	415.2, 417.2
Marshals	163.2, 162.7875, 164.6
Fisheries	163.225

NTSB	165.7625, 166.175
Postal Insp	162.225, 164.5, 169.85, 410.2, 413.6
State Dept	401.625, 407.6, 408.6, 407.2

NATIONAL RECREATION FREQUENCIES

In addition to specific team and stadium frequencies listed in the state information, here are a few interesting groups that operate or entertain nationwide, or travel from state to state.

Similar operations are likely to be licensed in the same general bands, so if you encounter a mobile performance which you'd like to monitor, scan near these frequencies and you'll probably find what you're looking for.

All American Circus	151.625
Barbara Mandrel Tour	154.6
Loretta Lynn	469.5, 469.55
Marshall Tucker Band	169.505
National Football League	461.2375, 461.3375, 461.5375, 461.7875, 464.1125, 464.3625, 464.7125, 464.9875, 466.2625, 466.4125, 466.7625, 466.8375, 461.4625, 461.6875, 461.8375
NRA Matches	467.6
Ringling Bros Circus	151.625, 153.02
Rodeo America	464.5, 464.55
U.S. Golf Ass'n	461.0375, 461.0875, 461.2625, 461.4625, 151.625, 464.55, 469.5, 469.55, 461.6125
U.S. Olympic Committee	462.625, 467.625
Olympic Torch Run	464.55
U.S. Ski Team	151.925, 151.955
U.S. Hockey Team	464.55
Women's Pro Golf Tour	464.5

ENOUGH'S ENOUGH! LET'S GET ROLLING

OK . . . you've programmed the military, national agency, and itinerant entertainer frequencies in which you're interested. But what about your cross-country route?

It would be nice to have a key to the laws of some of the more restrictive states, plus a block of useful frequencies for each state (especially those used by the highway patrol).

It would be even nicer to have frequencies for all of the major cities you're likely to pass through. Read on!

The Law

Every state has enacted legislation which, in various ways, says that if you voluntarily divert your attention from the business of driving, any resulting accident is your fault. Some states have gone further and prohibited certain things and activities which *might* divert your attention (for instance, television sets must be installed in such a manner that the screen cannot be seen by the driver).

Legislation prohibiting your mobile scanner is generally justified by three arguments. First, you might become so involved with what you hear that your driving becomes more dangerous. Second, you might hear something that leads you to an emergency situation at which the authorities would rather maintain their "exclusive." And third, a scanner might help you make your getaway.

Here's a guide prepared by Fran Olson [WB9ULS] and reprinted with permission. Where you see blanks, we simply don't have the information. The authors, publisher and Fran accept no responsibility for either errors in this list or changes in the law.

	RD	MS		RD	MS
ALABAMA	YES	YES	MONTANA	YES	YES
ALASKA	YES	YES	NEBRASKA	YES	YES
ARIZONA	YES	YES	NEVADA	YES	YES
ARKANSAS	YES	YES	NEW HAMPSHIRE	YES	YES
CALIFORNIA	YES	YES	NEW JERSEY	YES	YES
COLORADO	YES	YES	NEW MEXICO	YES	YES
CONNECTICUT	NO	YES	NEW YORK	NO	YES
DELAWARE	YES	YES	NORTH CAROLINA	YES	YES
DC	NO	...	NORTH DAKOTA	YES	YES
FLORIDA	YES	YES	OHIO	YES	YES
GEORGIA	YES	YES	OKLAHOMA	YES	...
HAWAII	YES	YES	OREGON	YES	YES
IDAHO	YES	YES	PENNSYLVANIA	YES	YES
ILLINOIS	YES	YES	RHODE ISLAND	YES	YES
INDIANA	YES	YES	SOUTH CAROLINA	YES	YES
IOWA	YES	YES	SOUTH DAKOTA	YES	YES
KANSAS	YES	YES	TENNESSEE	YES	YES
KENTUCKY	YES	YES	TEXAS	YES	YES
LOUISIANA	YES	YES	UTAH	YES	YES
MAINE	YES	YES	VERMONT	YES	...
MARYLAND	YES	YES	VIRGINIA	NO	YES
MASSACHUSETTS	YES	YES	WASHINGTON	YES	YES
MICHIGAN	YES	YES	WEST VIRGINIA	YES	YES
MINNESOTA	YES	YES	WISCONSIN	YES	YES
MISSISSIPPI	YES	YES	WYOMING	YES	YES
MISSOURI	YES	YES			

RD = Radar Detectors   MS = Mobile Scanners

Clubs

They're all over the country, with at least one in nearly every state. Scanner hobbyists congregate, share information, and take great pride in their knowledge of their particular "turf." Remember, typical scanning is in VHF and UHF, so a hobbyist with a monitoring station in his home is probably completely expert on everything within line of sight.

How can you gain access to that information? The following list was compiled from several inputs, and is a guide only. We *know* it is incomplete, and that there are errors! There is no practical way to canvass all states to generate a complete list.

The list is in alphabetical order by name of each group, so you have to look closely to pick out the state or city of interest to each of them.

All Ohio Scanner Club
Dave Marshall
50 Villa Rd.
Springfield, OH
45503-1036

Bay Area Scanner Enthusiasts
105 Serra Way #363
Milpitas, CA 95035

Bearcat Radio Club
PO Box 291918
Kettering, OH 45429

Capitol Hill Monitors
Alan Henney
6912 Prince Georges Ave
Takoma Park, MD
20912-5414

Central FL Listeners Group
956 Woodrose Court
Altamonte Springs, FL 32714-1261

Central VA Enthusiasts
Allen Cole
POB 34832
Richmond, VA 23234-0832

Chicago Area Radio Monitoring Association (CARMA)
Ted & Kim Moran
6536 N. Francisco 3E
Chicago, IL 60645

Cincinnati Area Monitoring Exchange (MONIX)

Mark Meece
7917 Third St.
West Chester, OH 45069

Communications Research Group
Scott Miller
122 Greenbriar Drive
Sun Prairie, WI 53590-1706

Houston Area Scanners and Monitoring Club
909 Michael
Alvin, TX 77511

Long Island Sounds
2134 Decker Ave
North Merrick, NY 11566

Metro Radio System
Julian Olansky
P.O. Box 26
Newton Highlands, MA 02161

Michigan Area Enthusiasts
P.O Box 81621
Rochester, MI 48308

Mountain NewsNet
James Richardson
P.O. Box 621124
Littleton, CO 80162-1124

NYC Radio Fre(ak)Qs
Joe Alverson
199 Barnard Ave
Staten Island, NY 10307

Northeast Scanner Club

Les Mattson
P .0. Box 62,
Gibbstown, NJ 08027

Radio Monitors of Maryland
Ron Bruckman
P.O. Box 394
Hampstead, MD 21074.

Rocky Mountain Listeners
Wayne Heinen
4131 S. Andes Way
Aurora, CO 80013-3831

Scanner/SWL SIG
Raleigh Amateur Radio Society
c/o Curt Phillips
P.O. Box 28587
Raleigh, NC 27611

Susquehanna City Scanner Club
P.O. Box 23
Prospect St.
Montrose, PA 18801

Toledo Area Radio Enthusiasts
Ernie Dellinger, N8PFA
6629 Sue Lane
Maumee, OH 43537

Triangle Area Scanner Listening Group
Curt Phillips, KD4YU
P.O. Box 28587
Raleigh, NC 27611

Wasatch Scanner Club

Jon Van Allen
2872 West 7140 South
West Jordan, UT 84084

Scanning Wisconsin
Ken Bitter
S. 67 W.
17912 Pearl Dr.
Muskego, WI 53150-9608

Internet
Frequency Sources

Here are some scattered Internet resources which have shown relative permanence. When planning a trip, visit the URLs (Web sites) shown and download frequency lists appropriate to your route.

Many of these Web sites also provide useful links to other lists (and so forth), and that's why they're "lumped together" rather than listed state-by-state.

In this listing, "http://www." is the preface unless otherwise designated.

The Boss!	**fcc.gov**
Public Safety	**geocities.com/capecanaveral/lab/**
Frequencies	**1060/natnlps.htm**
ID Boise Valley	cyberhighway.net/~relliott/freqs.ht ml
IN Evansville	comsource.net/~anderson/
New England	channel1.com/users/brennick/
	scanner.html
OH Cleveland	http://w3.gwis.com/~schilig/scanner.txt
PA (western)	geocities.com/capecanaveral/lab/
	1060/index.html
PA Philadelphia	geocities.com/capecanaveral/1273/
	scanner.html

CA (southern)	http://w6trw.sp.trw.com/scma/freq.htm
TN Knoxville	geocities.com/capecanaveral/lab/ 1060/knoxtn.htm
WI Green Bay	sparknet.net/~jtenor/list1.html
Newsgroups	alt.radio.scanner, rec.radio.scanner

Speed Traps

WHY?

Most of those who have worked at the local and city government level acknowledge that traffic tickets are an important source of revenue and provide a critical part of the budget. If our communities depend upon traffic fines to pay for key services, why did the authors decide to give you a little help in avoiding them?

Because our book gives you plenty of distractions, and we wanted to balance the equation. After all, if you weren't busy listening to your scanner (with our help) you probably would have noticed that speed limit sign and would not have gotten a ticket in the first place. Therefore, our attitude is that we're not denying the local treasuries a nickel!

OUR FILING SYSTEM

We've lumped the speed traps into one location rather than distributing them state by state, because so many of them are near a state's border. That's no accident, of course. You're cruising along Highway 237 in Tennessee at the posted limit of 65, but when you cross the border into Alabama there are two things waiting for you: a 55 mph sign, and a state patrolman, and they're both behind the bushes.

CB

We recommend listening to trucking channels on citizens band, because the professional driver is faced with an interesting challenge: speed is "positive" money, but a speeding ticket is "negative" money. His job is to maintain a profitable balance, so he communicates with his peers to expand the intelligence system. The one CB term to which you should be especially sensitive is "Smokey." Here are a few other key terms that will help you decipher the truckers' CB lingo:

Smokey	Highway patrolman, state trooper
Local	City or township policeman
County Mountie	Sheriff
Plain brown wrapper	Unmarked cruiser
Taking pictures	Radar
Clean shot to XXX	No law ahead (but to whom was that trucker talking, and which way was he going?)
Handle	Callsign.
Come back	The same as "over" in a WWII B-29

Unless you're female (and 95%+ of scanner hobbyists aren't), truckers will rarely talk to you. On the other hand, if you listen carefully to truckers you might get away with an imitation, particularly if you're in trouble. To improve your chances of initiating some sort of dialog, begin with news of a smokey, etc.

TRAPS

First, remember this: having foreknowledge of a customary law enforcement observation area does NOT give you a license to speed! Neither the authors, the publisher, nor the people who have reported these traps take responsibility for (1) our failure to warn you of a particular trap, or (2) the extra time it takes for you to get from point A to point B at the speed limit because you expected to find a patrol car there (but none was seen).

It's a good idea to monitor the local fuzz, using the frequencies provided in the state-by-state listings. Pay attention to the mile markers along the road, as they're used as a reference both by law enforcement and truckers. Here are a few of the more blatant speed traps reported in the last few years. "Reported" by whom? By the AAA, fellow scanner enthusiasts, trucker groups, Internet discussions, and other sources. NONE will take responsibility for errors.

State	Location	Comments
AL	Auburn Univ	Anything close to the campus
CA	Hwy 101 near Newport Beach	High-paying taxpayers demanded it
CA	Near Disneyland	Disneyland is the biggest taxpayer in the area, and wants to protect its reputation
CA	San Diego I-5 and I-805	From the Mexican border to downtown
CA	San Diego I-8	Right across the state, from the Pacific to the Arizona border
CA	San Francisco	Between the airport and downtown
CT	Westport I-95	Heavy fines, too
DC	Beltway	Goes through several states with hungry budgets
FL	Jacksonville I-10	Radar and heavy fines
FL	Melbourne Hwy 1	The treasuries of these little towns really need help, so the speed limit jumps around
FL	Santa Rosa Hwy 90 and nearby streets	Near Pensacola. White sand, lotsa sun, and many tickets to the gawking tourists
GA	Loganville Hwy 78	Better revenue than peanuts!
IL	National City State Hwy 3	Infamous!
IL	Springfield I-55	Another infamous speedtrap

IN	Kokomo Hwy 31	The AAA says so!
MA	Beltway 128	Solving the budget problem with the help of visitors
MA	Lexington everywhere	Unless you have a Raytheon sticker, walk, don't drive!
MD	Baltimore I-83	From the center of town to the northern arc of the beltway.
MD	Baltimore-DC Hwy 295	Especially near Laurel and the BWI airport
MT	All interstates	As of May 1999, 75 mph speed limit
MS	Pascagoula	If you're heading for Biloxi to gamble, don't speed by even 5 mph
NC	Jacksonville All areas	Especially if you have a Camp Lejeune (Marines) sticker on your car
NJ	Turnpike	Troopers have zero tolerance
NM	Hwy 54	Its entire length
NY	Long Island Southern Xpr	More patrols per mile than the Long Island Expressway
NV	Near all CA entry points	And, of course, if you're leaving NV you're probably broke!
OH	Dayton I-75	Stick to the posted limit, and stay wary
OK	Oklahoma City I-35	A great source of revenue
RI	Toll roads	They're timed! If you get where you're going too soon, you'll be fined at the exit.
TX	Patton Village Hwy 59	Terrible! And worse, most cars have weapons in them and the troopers act accordingly.
WV	Friendly State Hwy 2	That's the town's name, but not the attitude

Fuzz Codes

It's not nearly enough to have just the frequency plan of the local police or highway patrol, because what you hear will at best make intermittent sense.

Therefore, we've tried to find a guide to police codes to help you figure out what's really going on. The following list has been bouncing around the Internet for some time; we don't know who originally compiled it so we cannot give credit, though it appears that the list applies specifically to the Los Angeles Police Department. Fuzz codes are area-specific; we checked a lot of these codes with local police and came to the conclusion that there is no single set of codes that applies nationwide, though you can be certain of a few of the simpler 10-codes — 10-4 is *always* translated as "Roger." This is a guide that should be useful in combination with the context of the message in which the code is overheard.

Code	Possible interpretation
187	Homicide
207	Kidnapping
207A	Kidnapping attempt
211	Armed robbery
217	Assault w/ intent to murder

220	Attempted rape
240	Assault
242	Battery
245	Assault w/ deadly weapon
261	Rape
261A	Attempted rape
288	Lewd conduct
311	Indecent exposure
314	Indecent exposure
390	Drunk
390D	Drunk unconscious
415	Disturbance
415C	Disturbance, children
415E	Disturbance, loud party
415F	Disturbance, family
415G	Disturbance, gang
417	Person w/ a gun
459	Burglary
459A	Burglar alarm ringing
470	Forgery
480	Hit-and-run (felony)
481	Hit-and-run (misdemeanor)
484	Petty theft
484PS	Purse snatch
487	Grand theft
488	Petty theft
502	Drunk driving
503	Auto theft
504	Tampering w/ vehicle
505	Reckless driving
507	Public nuisance
586	Illegal parking
586E	Vehicle blocking driveway
594	Malicious mischief
595	Runaway car
647	Lewd conduct
901	Ambulance call/accident, inj unk

901A .... Ambulance call — attempted suicide
901H .... Ambulance call — dead body
901K .... Ambulance has been dispatched
901L .... Ambulance call — narcotics OD
901N .... Ambulance requested
901S .... Ambulance call — shooting
901T .... Ambulance call — traffic accident
901Y .... Request ambulance if needed
902 .... Accident
902H .... Enroute to hospital
902M .... Medical aid requested
902T .... Traffic accident — non-injury
903 .... Aircraft crash
903L .... Low flying aircraft
904A .... Fire alarm
904B .... Brush or boat fire
904C .... Car fire
904F .... Forest fire
904G .... Grass fire
904I .... Illegal burning
904S .... Structure fire
905B .... Animal bite
905N .... Noisy animal
905S .... Stray animal
905V .... Vicious animal
906K .... Rescue dispatched
906N .... Rescue requested
907 .... Minor disturbance
907A .... Loud radio or TV
907B .... Ball game in street
907K .... Paramedics dispatched
907N .... Paramedics requested
907Y .... Are paramedics needed?
908 .... Begging
909 .... Traffic congestion
909B .... Road blockade
909F .... Flares needed

909T .... Traffic hazard
910 .... Can you handle?
911 .... Advise party
911B .... Contact informant/contact officer
912 .... Are we clear?
913 .... You are clear
914 .... Request detectives
914A .... Attempted suicide
914C .... Request coroner
914D .... Request doctor
914F .... Request fire dept.
914H .... Heart attack
914N .... Concerned party notified
914S .... Suicide
915 .... Dumping rubbish
916 .... Holding suspect
917A .... Abandoned vehicle
917P .... Hold vehicle for fingerprints
918A .... Escaped mental patient
918V .... Violent mental patient
919 .... Keep the peace
920 .... Missing adult
920A .... Found adult/Missing adult
920C .... Missing child
920F .... Found child
920J .... Missing juvenile
921 .... Prowler
921P .... Peeping Tom
922 .... Illegal peddling
924 .... Station detail
925 .... Suspicious person
926 .... Request tow truck
926A .... Tow truck dispatched
927 .... Investigate unknown trouble
927A .... Person pulled from phone
927D .... Investigate posible dead body
928 .... Found property

929 .... Investigate person down
930 .... See man with complaint
931 .... See woman with complaint
932 .... Woman/child abuse
933 .... Open window
949 .... Gasoline spill
950 .... Burning permit
951 .... Request fire investigator
952 .... Report condititions
953 .... Check smoke report
954 .... Arrived at scene
955 .... Fire under control
956 .... Available for assignment
957 .... Fire under control
960X .... Car stop — dangerous suspects
961 .... Take a report
962 .... Subject is armed & dangerous
966 .... Sniper
967 .... Outlaw motorcyclists
975 .... Can suspect hear your radio?
981 .... Frequency is clear
982 .... Are we being received?
983 .... Explosion
995 .... Labor trouble
996 .... Explosion
996A .... Unexploded bomb
998 .... Officer involved in shooting
999 .... Officer needs help - urgent!
10-1 .... You are being received poorly
10-2 .... You are being received ok
10-3 .... Stop transmitting/Change channels
10-4 .... OK, acknowledgement, "Roger"
10-5 .... Relay
10-6 .... Station is busy, standby unless urgent
10-7 .... Out of serv, radio off (w/ location+phone)
10-8 .... In service
10-9 .... Repeat last message

10-10	Out of service — radio on
10-11	Transmitting too fast
10-12	Visitors present
10-13	Advise weather and road conditions
10-14	Convoy or escort detail
10-15	Enroute to jail w/prisoner
10-16	Pick up prisoner
10-17	Pick up papers
10-18	Complete assignment quickly
10-19	Go to your station, or I'm enroute to mine
10-20	Location (My 20 is..., or What's your 20?)
10-21	Telephone your station
10-22	Disregard, cancel last message
10-23	Stand by
10-24	Trouble at station
10-27	Check computer for warrants
10-28	Check for full info on vehicle or suspect
10-29	Check/advise if vehicle/subject is wanted
10-30	Subject has no record, no wants
10-31	Subject has record, but no wants
10-32	Subject is wanted
10-33	Emergency traffic in the air
10-34	Clearance for emergency message
10-35	Backup needed
10-36	Correct time
10-36	Correct time/Confidential info
10-37	Correct time
10-39	Message delivered
10-87	Meet an officer
10-97	Arriving at assigned detail
10-98	Assigned detail complete
10-99	Emergency — all units and stations!
11-6	Illegal discharge of firearms
11-7	Prowler
11-8	Person down
11-10	Take a report
11-12	Dead animal or loose livestock

11-13	Injured animal
11-14	Animal bite
11-15	Ball game in street
11-17	Wires down
11-24	Abandoned vehicle
11-25X	Female motorist needs assistance
11-27	Subject has record, no wants
11-28	Rush vehicle information information
11-29	Subject has no record, no wants
11-30	Incomplete phone call
11-31	Person calling for help
11-40	Advise if ambulance needed
11-41	Request ambulance
11-42	Ambulance not req/Paramedics needed
11-43	Doctor required
11-44	Possible fatality
11-45	Attempted suicide
11-46	Death report
11-47	Injured person
11-48	Provide transportation
11-50	Field interrogation
11-51	Security check
11-70	Fire alarm
11-71	Fire report
11-78	Paramedics dispatched
11-79	Traffic accident — ambulance dispatched
11-80	Traffic accident — serious injury
11-81	Traffic accident — minor injury
11-82	Traffic accident — property damaged
11-83	Traffic accident — no details
11-84	Direct traffic
11-85	Send tow truck
11-86	Special detail/Bomb threat
11-87	Bomb found
11-88	Assist motorist
11-98	Meet an officer
11-99	Officer needs help — Urgent!

YOU'RE READY!

Now that you're properly armed, equipped, trained, warned, and funded, and you have your personal translation dictionaries, the next sections will tell you how to tune your scanner on your next vacation.

State by State

ALABAMA

Forestry/Conservation   159.42, 159.345, 159.465, 155.01,
and Fish/Game   159.315, 151.43, 151.28, 168.725

Recreation, Tourism, Parks,
Forests, and Monuments

Bankhead National Forest	168.725, 169.325
Conecuh National Forest	168.725
Horseshoe Bend	172.45
Natchez Parkway	171.675
Talladega National Forest	168.725, 171.425
Talladega Speedway	464.775, 469.775
USS Alabama	155.655
State Police	158.79, 159.03, 154.92,
	155.445, 155.010

Cities: Emergency Services

Birmingham   Trunked 851-866, 460.3, 460.175,

	460.475, 460.075, 460.375,
	460.15, 154.19, 155.34
Huntsville	154.815, 155.25, 155.415,155.85,
	155.01, 154.415, 462.975
Mobile	Trunked 856-869
Montgomery	460.5, 460.025, 460.35,855.2375,
	855.7125 154.43, 154.385

ALASKA

Forestry/Conservation	453.1, 453.15, 453.2, 453.3,
	453.35, 453.4, 453.45, 453.5
Fish/Game	45.04, 45.0, 151.19, 151.25,
	159.27

Recreation, Tourism, Parks, Forests, and Monuments

Denali National Park	166.3
Glacier Bay National Park	156.45, 156.6, 156.8
Klondike Gold Rush	166.3, 166.95
Sitka Historic Park	30.1
Tongass National Forest	164.125, 164.825, 168.625
Wrangell-St Elias	166.77
State Troopers	155.25, 155.79, 155.73,
	155.415, 155.25

Cities: Emergency Services

Anchorage	155.01, 155.43, 155.64,
	460.05, 460.1, 460.15, 460.25,
	460.3, 154.31, 154.445, 155.16,
	155.385
Fairbanks	155.01, 154.205, 154.43,
	155.16, 155.28
Juneau	156.21, 158.88, 155.13,
	154.965, 154.25, 155.22, 155.295

ARIZONA

Forestry/Conservation	164.875, 166.9, 168.35, 169.6, 169.9, 169.95, 170.05, 172.45, 172.575
Fish/Game	151.385, 151.4, 151.415, 151.43, 151.445, 151.46, 151.475, 151.49
Canyon de Chelly	166.35, 166.95
Casa Grande Ruins	168.35, 163.125, 169.4
Glen Canyon	164.875, 171.625, 172.4
Grand Canyon Area	172.575
Kaibab National Forest	170.55, 169.9
Lake Mead	166.9, 166.3, 166.35
Montezuma Castle	168.5
Navajo National Monument	166.35, 171.675, 172.575
Painted Desert	170.05
Petrified Forest	170.05
Saguaro	166.35, 166.95
Sunset Crater	166.35, 166.95
Walnut Canyon	164.425, 166.3, 166.9
State Highway Patrol	460.475, 460.025, 460.3, 460.4, 460.325, 460.425, 464.225

Cities: Emergency Services

Grand Canyon	155.49, 151.4, 155.835, 155.13, 159.21, 155.64, 154.385, 154.355, 154.19
Phoenix	154.89, 155.37, 155.07, 155.64, 156.06, 155.61, 453.1, 453.2, 453.675, 154.19, 154.25, 154.31
Tucson	155.01, 155.73, 154.725, 155.49, 155.85, 154.875, 155.19, 453.1, 453.2, 453.3, 203.5

ARKANSAS

Forestry/Conservation	151.205, 151.22, 151.25, 151.295, 168.625, 169.675, 169.9, 171.575
Fish/Game	151.175, 151.34, 151.385, 159.33, 159.42

Recreation, Tourism, Parks, Forests, and Monuments

Arkansas Post National	166.325
Buffalo National River	164.75
Fort Smith Historic Site	164.75
Hot Springs National Park	166.325
Pea Ridge Mil Park	168.325
State Police	856.9375, 857.7625, 858.7625, 859.7625, 857.9375, 858.9375, 856.8125, 857.8125

Cities: Emergency Services

Fort Smith	453.65, 453.75, 453.65, 453.75, 453.95, 453.85, 461.6, 462.95, 462.975
Hot Springs	155.415, 155.445, 158.97, 159.05, 154.34, 153.77, 155.88
Little Rock	Trunked 856-861, 453.05, 453.35, 453.225, 453.8, 453.95, 462.95

CALIFORNIA

Forestry/Conservation	151.265, 151.355, 164.125, 164.75, 164.825,166.125, 168.125, 168.625, 168.65, 171.575, 172.650,
Fish/Game	151.41, 151.415, 151.43

Recreation, Tourism, Parks, Forests, and Monuments

Anaheim Stadium	461.65, 460.15, 455.675
Anza-Borrego	858.125
Big Sur	855.9625
Cabrillo Monument	171.75
Candlestick	855.7375
Clear Lake	855.7125
Death Valley	170.1
Diablo	855.9625
Disneyland	464.325, 464.6375, 464.4875
Golden Gate Rec Area	162.6125, 164.0, 164.525
Goldmines	855.7125
Joshua Tree	171.675
Klamath	857.9375
Knotts Berry Farm	151.655, 462.1625, 151.625
LA Universal Studios	151.895, 152.9, 152.87
Lake Tahoe	172.25, 415.45, 419.15
Magic Mountain	151.895, 151.955, 154.54
Monterey	855.9625, 855.7125
Napa Valley	855.7125
Pendleton Coast	856.125
Plumas/Eureka	857.9375
Redwood National Park	165.1625
Salton Sea	858.125
San Diego Coast	855.125
SD Qualcomm Stad	151.925, 151.685, 464.1
SD Sea World	154.515, 154.540, 156.35

SD Wild Animal Park	453.2, 453.35
SD Zoo	151.895, 154.57, 461.0125
SF Embarcadero	854.8375
Sierra National Forest	169.125, 171.4, 171.475
Sequoia National Forest	164.75, 168.175, 168.675
Warner Bros Studio	461.0625, 461.5625
Yosemite	172.65, 172.755, 172.625
Highway Patrol	42.12, 42.2, 42.66, 42.72,
	42.28, 42.44, 42.4, 42.16,
	42.46, 42.7, 42.48, 42.68,
	42.5, 42.82, 42.52, 42.3,
	42.08
CHP Academy	42.5
CHP Common & A/C	42.34, 42.18

Cities: Emergency Services

Bakersfield	155.31, 154.8, 155.19,
	154.74, 154.07
Fresno	460.05, 160.325, 460.275,
	460.4, 453.55, 153.845
Irvine (Orange County)	460.425, 460.525, 507.1125
Los Angeles	Drive-by shootings: 154.83
	484.2875—484.9625, 25kHz
	506.3625—507.1375, 25kHz
	859.4375, 858.4375,
	868.9875, 857.9375,
	856.2375
Riverside	460.175, 460.325, 460.6,
	460.3, 460.575
San Diego	856—864 MHz, 25 kHz steps
	857—860 MHz, 25 kHz steps
	158.73, 158.97, 159.09,
	159.045, 154.31, 154.415,
	153.785, 155.025, 155.175
San Francisco	45.1, 45.14, 460.225,
	460.125, 460.5, 460.075,
	123.025(a/c), 122.875(a/c),
	488.3625, 488.5625, 453.15,

	488.7625, 155.385, 158.76
Sacramento	460.05, 460.2, 460.325,
	460.475, 153.95, 153.89
	Trunked 866—869
San Jose	460.2, 460.325, 460.425,
	460.4, 460.475, 154.01
Santa Barbara	460.1, 460.325, 460.05,
	460.55, 154.445, 155.775

COLORADO

Forestry/Conservation and Fish/Game	168.625, 169.175, 164.125, 151.145, 151.19, 151.175, 164.125, 169.9, 164.15, 166.35

Recreation, Tourism, Parks, Forests, and Monuments

Black Canyon	166.3, 166.35
CO National Monument	166.3
Dinosaur National Mon	166.375
Florissant Fossil Beds	167.025
Great Sand Dunes	166.35, 173.7625
Mesa Verde	170.05
Rocky Mtn National Park	166.35, 166.95, 168.35
State Patrol	
Statewide Simplex	154.905
NLEEC	155.475
	154.74, 155.445, 154.755, 155.445, 154.74, 154.695, 154.83, 159.09, 155.505, 154.77, 156.21, 155.505, 154.83, 155.31
Control freqs	154.935, 154.695, 154.845, 154.905

Cities: Emergency Services

Aspen	155.25, 155.85, 153.845, 155.595, 154.325, 155.34
Colorado Springs	453.75, 453.85, 453.55, 460.625, 154.13, 462.975, Trunked 854—861
Denver Trunked	855—867, 453.1, 453.45, 453.775, 154.31
Fort Collins	460.3, 460.35, 460.6, 855.9625
Vail	453.1, 453.8, 460.425, 453.4, 453.15, 155.16

CONNECTICUT

Forestry/Conservation and Fish/Game	44.68, 44.72, 44.76, 44.92, 151.175, 151.385

Recreation, Tourism, Parks, Forests, and Monuments

Bridgeport Jai Alai	151.715
CT Int'l Raceway	154.57
Maritime Center	467.0625
Milford Jai Alai	157.74
Mystic Seaport Museum	464.575, 464.6
Stafford Speedway	464.5, 154.54
Waterford Speed Bowl	151.625
State Police	154.83, 154.665, 154.65, 154.695, 155.475, 42.04, 42.36, 42.48, 42.52,
Radar Squad	42.2, 42.24

Cities: Emergency Services

Bridgeport	154.725, 155.43, 155.77, 153.77, 463.575
Hartford	Trunked 856—867, 154.31,

	462.95, 154.265
New Haven	460.45, 460.5, 851.0125, 47.5
New London	453.275, 460.05, 453.9

DELAWARE

Forestry/Conservation	159.225, 159.42, 44.92
	31.98, 151.175, 151.385
Fish/Game	44.68, 44.72, 45.28

Recreation, Tourism, Parks, Forests, and Monuments

Davison Racing	464.1875
Delaware Park	151.655
Dover Downs	467.825, 469.550, 463.9
State Police	154.665, 154.77, 154.935,
	154.65, 154.755, 154.71,
	154.86, 45.02, 44.86,
	465.475

Cities: Emergency Services

| Dover | 155.31, 156.7, 154.86, |
| | 153.935, 146.2, 33.78 |

DISTRICT OF COLUMBIA

| **Forestry/Conservation** | 166.725, 166.925, 166.85, |
| **and Fish/Game** | 166.95, 409.05, 417.975, 172.75 |

Recreation, Tourism, Parks, Forests, and Monuments

Capitol Center	461.675
Convention Center	453.1125
DC Zoo	172.475
Hillwood Museum	154.57

JFK Center	409.050
National Visitor Center	411.925
RFK Stadium	464.375
Smithsonian	169.2, 165.0375, 169.0375
Special Olympics	465.8
U. S. Capitol Police	169.225, 169.5375, 170.175, 162.25, 162.6125, 163.1

Cities: Emergency Services

Washington	460.35, 460.25, 460.025, 460.325, 154.19, 154.235, 852.6125, 192.8, 460.2

FLORIDA

Forestry/Conservation	159.3, 159.33, 159.27, 159.405, 159.45, 159.375, 172.525, 172.775, 172.425, 164.825
Fish/Game	151.385(pri), 151.415, 160.14, 160.425, 161.445, 172.275, 151.31, 151.43, 159.285, 44.76

Recreation, Tourism, Parks, Forests, and Monuments

Amish Homestead	151.625
Apalachicola Nat'l Forest	164.825
Busch Gardens	461.7125, 462.0875
Big Cypress Preserve	172.425
Biscayne National Park	172.675
Canaveral Seashore	164.75
Daytona Speedway	154.515, 154.54, 464.9
Disney World	463.75, 462.55, 463.975
Everglades National Park	172.525, 172.775
Fort Caroline Memorial	170.05
Fort Jefferson Monument	171.2625, 168.55

Gulf Islands National Seas	171.525, 171.725, 172.525
Kennedy Space Ctr	164.75, 165.1125, 173.6875
Miami Metro Zoo	471.2625, 471.2875
National Wildlife Refuge	462.7
Ocala National Forest	164.825, 168.675, 169.9
Osceola National Forest	164.825, 164.125
PGA Golf Club	151.955
Sea World of FL	151.805, 154.6, 464.775
Six Flags, Hollywood	151.775
St Augustine Alligator Park	151.925
Treasure Island	464.5
Universal Studios	451.75, 461.2875, 461.8875
Yogi Bear Jellystone	151.865
State Highway Patrol	155.665, 154.68, 154.695, 155.92, 155.37, 465.1625, 45.06, 453.575, 453.625, 156.18, 155.37

Cities: Emergency Services

Daytona Beach	Trunked 866—869
Fort Lauderdale	Trunked 866—869, 460.05, 460.1, 460.125, 470.6125, 471.1375
Jacksonville	Trunked 855—861, 453.15, 453.1, 453.05, 460.575, 462.975
Key West	Trunked 853—867, 154.725, 154.755, 154.65, 460.6, 45.2
Miami	Trunked 854—861, 453.1, 453.425
Miami Beach	Trunked 856—861 460.525, 460.55
Orlando	460.05, 460.1, 460.4, 851.3875, 851.4125, 851.4375, 851.4625, 851.4875, 851.8375, 860.9625, 860.9875,

	453.05, 154.43, 154.16,
	154.25, 462.95
Pensacola	460.425, 460.175, 154.37,
	460.6, 460.575, 155.895,
	460.1, 460.45
St. Petersburg	Trunked 856—861
Tallahassee	460.025, 460.125, 460.225,
	154.19, 154.385, 462.95
Tampa	453.55, 453.7, 453.325,
	154.43, 462.975, 155.22

GEORGIA

Forestry/Conservation	31.14. 31.22
Fish/Game	31.1
Recreation, Tourism, Parks,	
Forests, and Monuments	
Atlanta Coliseum	151.655
Atlanta Center	464.575
Atlanta Raceway	464.075
Atlanta Symphony	151.625
Atlanta Braves	464.325
Chattahoochee Park	168.775, 166.3
Cumberland Island	171.525
Georgia State Fair	461.2875, 461.4625
ML King Historic Site	408.475
Oconee National Forest	168.775
Science/Tech Museum	464.825
Six Flags	462.05, 462.1, 464.575
Stone Mtn National Park	853.8125, 855.0125
State Patrol	154.68, 154.8, 155.91,
	155.475, 154.905, 154.935,
	155.37, 458.4875

Cities: Emergency Services
Albany   460.375, 460.175, 154.355

	155.235, 460.05, 155.16
Athens	154.83, 155.52, 155.295
Atlanta	Trunked 851-861, 853.1125,
	852.4625, 852.9625, 154.19,
	153.89, 462.95
Augusta	460.3, 154.34, 158.745
Savannah	Trunked 856-861, 460.025,
	154.31, 155.16

HAWAII

Forestry/Conservation	141.975,151.925, 154.995,
and Fish/Game	168.55, 169.55, 408.575,
	453.7, 464.5625

**Recreation, Tourism, Parks,
Forests, and Monuments**

Bishop Museum	154.57
Diamond Head Memorial	464.5625
Haleakala National Park	169.55
Kailua Windsurfing	151.955
Kona Watersports	461.25
Lucky Lik Fishing	462.075
Movie Production	173.225
PGA Honolulu	154.54
Polynesian Cultural C	154.54
Sea Life Park	33.4
Skip Barber Racing	463.775
USS Arizona	408.575
Volcanos National Park	168.55
Waikiki Yacht Club	464.3
Waimea	151.925
Windjammer Cruises	464.15
Police (for all islands)	Trunked 856-861

Cities/Islands — Emergency Services

Hilo	155.61, 155.535, 154.385

Honolulu	155.19, 155.685, 155.52,
	154.22, 453.925, 453.7
Kawaii	155.85, 154.43, 453.4
Maui	155.73, 155.55, 453.25

IDAHO

Forestry/Conservation	159.225, 159.36, 163.375, 168.75,
	169.6, 171.45, 171.675, 172.2
Fish/Game	151.145, 153.845, 159.285,
	159.315, 159.39, 159.450

**Recreation, Tourism, Parks,
Forests, and Monuments**

Appaloosa Horse Club	464.5
Bitter Root	168.75
Bridger	169.125
Caribou	171.475
Challis	169.6
Coeur d'Alene Grayhound	467.7625
Craters of the Moon	171.675
Hell's Canyon	163.375
Humboldt	169.9
Idaho State Fair	154.57
Kaniksu	168.775
Magic Mtn Ski Patrol	155.295
Meridian Speedway	462.0375
Payette	164.6, 168.65, 171.55
Salmon	165.4125, 164.6, 171.6
Sun Valley Ski Guides	157.59, 154.515
Teton	169.125
State Police	460.1, 460.2, 460.525,
	460.025, 460.3

Cities: Emergency Services

Boise	453.3, 453.35, 154.37,
	453.575, 155.385, 155.34

Pocatello	460.175, 154.445, 153.77
Twin Falls	460.5, 460.575, 155.4

ILLINOIS

Forestry/Conservation   151.250, 151.280, 151.445
and Fish/Game
Recreation, Tourism, Parks,
Forests, and Monuments

Adler Planetarium	469.875
Aero Adventures	151.835
Arlington Park Raceway	151.625, 464.55, 464.9
Boone County Fair	464.55
Brookfield Zoo	154.6, 155.115, 463.6875
Calumet Raceway	154.57
Chicago Bears	151.625
Chicago Cubs	464.5875, 151.685
Chicago White Sox	151.835
Chicago Stadium	151.925
Great America	464.875, 463.5375
Hollywood Riverboat	464.375
Illinois State Fair	155.46, 158.865, 42.5
Museum of Sci & Industry	464.55, 469.825
Playboy Enterprises	464.35
PGA Illinois	464.55
Raceway Park	154.6
Sears Tower	462.9
Sportsman's Park	461.4875, 461.925
Illinois Dept. of	42.52, 42.62, 42.72, 42.56, 42.88,
Law Enforcement	42.34, 42.66, 42.36, 155.52,
	154.935, 154.695, 154.665,
	154.68, 42.6, 42.7
Aircraft	42.5, 155.46, 122.975

Cities: Emergency Services
Bloomington   453.15, 453.1, 154.16,

Champaign	453.025, 453.25, 453.4, 154.25, 155.61, 453.625
Chicago	Trunked 865-869, 460.575, 460.05, 154.13, 155.77, 460.6, 460.65
Peoria	460.05, 154.145, 460.225
Springfield	Trunked 856-861, 460.4, 460.425, 158.745, 460.575

INDIANA

Forestry/Conservation	155.445, 159.24, , 159.345, 159.435, 164.825, 166.325
Fish/Game	159.225, 159.465

Recreation, Tourism, Parks, Forests, and Monuments

Dunes National Lakeshore	166.325, 166.275
General Motors Speedway	158.28, 462.3
Hoosier National Forest	164.825, 164.125
Indianapolis Speedway	151.685, 151.625, 154.6
Lincoln Boyhood	168.35
Paragon Speedway	151.625, 154.57
Speedrome	462.625, 462.675
State Fair	453.6
TriState Speedway	154.57, 151.655
TwinCities Speedway	151.625, 154.57
Wawasee Ski Area	154.6
Winchester Speedway	154.6, 155.34
State Police	42.42, 42.26, 42.4, 42.12, 42.16, 42.32, 155.455, 155.475, 453.05

Cities: Emergency Services

Bloomington	460.325, 154.415, 155.22
Elkhart	155.58, 154.43, 155.295
Evansville	Trunked 856-861, 855.4875, 855.9875, 154.22, 155.34

Fort Wayne	155.535, 155.79, 154.325
Indianapolis	Trunked 854-868
South Bend	453.65, 154.19, 155.34

IOWA

Forestry/Conservation   155.595, 45.0
Fish/Game   453.65
**Recreation, Tourism, Parks,
Forests, and Monuments**

Adventureland	464.525
Boone RR Museum	463.8
Clay Cty Fair	151.895
Des Moines Conv Ctr	464.975
Des Moines Skywalk	151.925
Eddyville Dragway	151.685
EmeraldLady Riverbo	151.925
Exp A/C Museum	464.55
Five Flags Dubuque	154.6
Ft Madison Rodeo	151.625
Prairie Meadows Race	461.85, 464.2
Riverboat Days	151.685, 151.895
State Fair	153.92
Sundown Ski Area	461.675
Vet Mem Auditorium	464.55
Highway patrol	155.64, 155.79, 155.655, 155.685, 155.565, 155.7, 155.37, 155.43, 155.67, 156.21, 155.91

Cities: Emergency Services

Cedar Rapids	460.175, 154.43, 155.34
Davenport	460.125, 460.575, 462.95
Des Moines	460.025, 460.4, 460.625, 460.575, 155.22, 450.45
Dubuque	460.375, 460.45, 154.13
Keokuk	155.13, 154.445

KANSAS

Forestry/Conservation	166.675
Fish/Game	39.20, 39.78, 39.58, 39.7, 453.725
Recreation, Tourism, Parks, Forests, and Monuments	
Boy Scouts	463.65
Eisenhower Library	415.2
Ft. Larned	170.05
Golf Courses/America	464.175
KS Expo Center	464.375, 464.525
Louisville Speedway	154.57, 154.6
Manhattan Zoo	151.16
Salina Bicentennial	151.955
Wichita Baseball	464.825
Highway patrol	44.98, 44.82, 44.94, 45.18, 45.14, 39.58, 39.46, 39.7
Turnpike Police	154.83, 154.68, 154.905
Cities: Emergency Services	
Dodge City	154.98, 154.31, 155.88
Lawrence	158.79, 154.4, 155.22
Topeka	460.475, 154.43, 462.975
Wichita	Trunked 856-861, 462.975, 854.9625

KENTUCKY

Forestry/Conservation	31.9, 31.66, 31.74, 453.925
Fish/Game	151.295, 151.175, 151.295, 151.145, 166.3, 166.7875, 169.55, 171.525

Recreation, Tourism, Parks, Forests, and Monuments

Beech Bend Park	462.65
Big South Fork	166.3
Churchill Downs	457.575, 461.8875, 462.787
Derby Museum	469.5375, 469.8875
Jockey Club	461.075
Keeneland Racetrack	154.6
Kentucky Derby Fest	154.6
Louisville Downs	151.625
Mammoth Cave	170.075, 464.875
Museum History/Sci	154.515, 154.54
Performing Arts Ctr	154.57, 461.7625
State Fair	153.875, 159.15
Zoological Park	464.425
State Police	453.85, 453.55, 453.45, 453.6, 453.3, 453.9, 453.95, 154.665, 155.475, 155.37

Cities: Emergency Services

Frankfort	155.625, 154.385, 158.97
Lexington	155.565, 463.0, 154.37
Louisville	460.025, 460.55, 462.95
Owensboro	155.73, 154.25, 155.205

LOUISIANA

Forestry/Conservation	151.325, 151.235, 151.145, 151.175, 151.25, 151.28, 151.385, 151.4, 856.2625
Fish/Game	31.06, 31.5, 31.22, 31.3, 31.38, 31.5, 31.86, 159.405

Recreation, Tourism, Parks, Forests, and Monuments

Boot Hill Speedway	151.625
Caddo Carrer Center	154.57

Capitol Dragway	154.57
Convention Center	462.475, 464.8875
Delta Queen	461.4, 464.85
Jean Lafitte National Park	169.675
Kisatchie National Forest	169.925, 164.9375
LA State Fair	154.57, 464.15, 464.975
Nantahala National Forest	171.475
New Orleans Saints	453.425, 453.775
NO Steamboat	461.975
Orpheum Theatre	463.625
Poydras Center	464.1125
Riverwalk	464.1125, 464.825
Saenger Perf Arts Ctr	461.0125
Shreveport Baseball	151.865
Superdome	453.425, 453.775
State police	155.505, 154.875, 158.97, 155.655, 155.565, 154.92, 154.935, 154.755, 154.905, 155.46, 154.695, 155.595, 159.315, 155.85, 155.91, 154.68, trunked 851-861

Cities: Emergency Services

Baton Rouge	Trunked 851-868, 155.61, 153.43, 155.67
New Orleans	Trunked 856-869
Shreveport	453.8, 453.9, 154.445

MAINE

Forestry/Conservation	159.36, 159.39, 159.42, 159.45, 159.33, 154.815, 151.265, 159.24, 159.3
Fish/Game	154.725, 155.97, 155.655, 155.595

Recreation, Tourism, Parks, Forests, and Monuments

Acadia National Park	164.175
Appalachian Mtn Club	463.95
Bar Harbor Camping	461.275
Booth Bay RR Museum	151.715
Chisholm Ski Club	464.325
Evergreen Valley Ski	155.175, 155.22
Katahdin Lodge	463.725
National Fishing Expo	464.5, 464.55, 469.5
Outward Bound Sch	154.540, 462.1
Oxford Speedway	151.625
Squaw Mtn Ski	154.6
Sugarloaf Mtn Club	154.54
White Mtn National Forest	170.575
State police	154.65, 154.655, 154.695, 154.71, 154.445, 155.505, 155.85, 154.935, 155.475, 156.045, 460.225, 452.45

Cities: Emergency Services

Augusta	155.19, 154.4, 155.235
Bangor	155.61, 154.22, 154.31
Brunswick	155.37, 154.34, 155.205
Kennebunkport	155.19, 33.7, 155.265
Portland	155.49, 154.205, 158.97

MARYLAND

Forestry/Conservation	151.46, 151.325, 151.145, 151.355, 151.415, 151.25,
Fish/Game	151.205, 159.24, 39.22, 39.2, 39.1

Recreation, Tourism, Parks, Forests, and Monuments

Annapolis Boat Show	154.6

Antietam Battlefield	166.95, 166.35
Assateague Seashore	170.05
Camden Yards	461.6375, 463.5625
Catoctin Mtn Park	171.725
C & O Canal	166.35
Capitol Raceway	154.6, 462.7
Columbia Parks/Recr	151.865, 154.54
Ft McHenry	166.95
Harborplace	461.825, 463.6625, 464.475
National Aquarium	464.825, 464.475, 464.975
Orioles	464.3625, 464.6375
Pimlico Racetrack	464.975
Wisp Ski Resort	461.8875, 462.1125
State police	39.1, 39.3, 39.34, 39.14, 39.32, 39.38, 39.24, 39.52, 39.04, 39.06, 39.22, 155.73, 453.55, 460.05

Cities: Emergency Services

Annapolis	Trunked 856-861, 494.5125, 463.175, 154.295
Baltimore	Trunked 856-861, 453.425, 453.275, 453.825, 154.31, 154.415, 154.145, 161.085
Ocean City	453.75, 460.5125, 154.325

MASSACHUSSETTS

Forestry/Conservation and Fish/Game	151.205, 151.145, 151.235, 151.31, 151.37, 31.46, 31.

Recreation, Tourism, Parks, Forests, and Monuments

Aquarium	484.0125
Big "E" Expo	154.6, 154.71
Boston Esplanade	151.28
Boston Garden	154.6, 154.57

Boston Marathon	464.1, 462.675, 461.5125
Boston Symphony	154.6, 461.1
Cape Cod Seashore	171.725
Firstnight	462.625, 464.55
Fogg Art Museum	484.8125
Gardner Museum	464.775
Great Woods Ctr	151.625, 151.805
Historical Park	166.775, 166.95
Lowell National Hist Park	166.95
Martha's Vineyard	156.35, 151.25, 151.355
Minuteman Historic Park	164.425
Museum of Fine Arts	151.745, 462.875
Museum of Science	151.625, 462.65
Patriots	154.57, 464.425
Raynham Dog Track	151.805, 464.0625
Red Sox	463.325, 464.075, 463.4125
Riverside Park	35.06, 464.925
Senior PGA Tour	151.625, 151.505
State police	42.44, 42.34, 42.4, 42.5, 42.54, 42.46, 42.42, 44.47, 44.9, 39.76, 39.8, 154.92, Trunked 856-861

Cities: Emergency Services

Amherst	460.15, 154.37, 460.175
Boston	460.35, 460.45, 460.3, 460.5, 460.125, 460.175, 483.1625, 453.65, 462.975
Cape Cod	155.565, 453.7, 463.1
Springfield	460.1, 460.45, 154.4
Worcester	Trunked 851-856

MICHIGAN

Forestry/Conservation	164.825, 169.925, 169.125, 168.125

Fish/Game   44.64, 44.72, 44.8, 44.84,
                                 44.88, 44.92, 151.295

Recreation, Tourism, Parks,
Forests, and Monuments

Alpine Valley Ski	151.835
Big Powderhorn Mountain	151.895
Chippewa Nature Center	157.56
Detroit Yacht Club	464.925
Detroit Zoo	151.205
Hiawatha National Forest	164.825
Huron National Forest	169.925
Indiana Dunes Lakeshore	166.325
Indianhead Mtn	151.655
Interlochen Art Center	151.715
Isle Royale National Park	169.675
Kalamazoo Speedway	151.625
Manistee National Forest	169.925
Michigan Spec Olympics	464.5, 464.55
Nubs Nob	157.68, 154.6
Olympia Stadium	154.57
Pontiac Silverdome	462.675
Renaissance Center	462.6, 463.9
Sleeping Bear Dunes	166.375
Space World	464.05, 462.7375
Spartan Speedway	151.685
State police	42.58, 42.74, 42.02, 42.64,
	42.68, 42.94, 42.48,
	154.695, 154.665, 154.68,
	155.37, 155.79, 155.445,
	155.595, 155.43, 155.565,
	460.175, 460.125
Aircraft	42.5, 42.48

Cities: Emergency Services

Battle Creek	154.815, 154.25, 155.535
Detroit	Trunked 851-856, 453.35,
	453.3, 453.75, 154.31, 155.76,
	123.075

Flint	155.07, 153.89, 155.16
Grand Rapids	155.655, 460.6, 155.16
Kalamazoo	Trunked 851-856, 155.685, 154.31, 155.16

MINNESOTA

Forestry/Conservation	151.265, 151.325, 151.385, 151.475, 154.295, 151.19, 151.145 - 151.495
Fish/Game	159.3, 151.265, 171.75, 172.45, 453.475

Recreation, Tourism, Parks, Forests, and Monuments

Aquatennial Parade	146.25, 148.15, 151.955
Buck Hill Ski	154.57, 851.6875
Canterbury Downs	158.46, 461.1625
Chippewa National Forest	164.825
Como Zoo	155.715
Duluth Alpine Club	151.655
Elko Speedway	154.6
Giant's Ridge Ski	151.955
Grand Portage Monument	166.325
Grand Prix Raceway	462.175
Humphrey Metrodome	464.575, 464.775, 155.025
Medieval Adventures	151.715
Minnesota Racetrack	158.46, 461.1625
Mt. Kato Ski	464.375
Quadna Mtn Resort	154.57
Renaissance Festival	151.715, 151.655
Scandinavia Today	154.57
St. Croix Riverway	164.25, 408.675, 411.725
St. Paul Civic Center	154.6
St. Paul Winter Carnival	151.625
State Fair	153.965

Sugar Hills Ski	151.745
Superior National Forest	169.925, 164.1, 166.675
Transportation Museum	151.625
Valley Fair	35.06, 35.1, 454.2625
Valley National Wildlife	171.750, 172.45
State patrol	154.92, 154.935, 154.665,
	154.68, 155.505, 158.91,
	159.36, 159.39, 159.42,
	158.91, 159.39, 159.21,
	159.345, 159.030
Aircraft / radar	171.575

Cities: Emergency Services

Duluth	155.595, 154.31, 155.4
Minneapolis	460.025, 460.1, 154.34,
	460.175, 155.4, 460.425
Rochester	155.58, 154.37, 155.235
St. Paul	460.05, 460.15, 460.575,
	460.6, 460.45, 460.375

MISSISSIPPI

Forestry/Conservation	151.145, 151.355, 151.475,
	168.675, 168.775, 171.425
Fish/Game	45.0, 45.04, 45.22

Recreation, Tourism, Parks, Forests, and Monuments

Bienville National Forest	168.675
Delta National Forest	168.675
DeSoto National Forest	168.675
Freedom Hall	154.54
Holly Springs	168.775
Homochitto	171.425
MS Coast Coliseum	453.375, 458.3375
MS/AL State Fair	151.895
Natchez Trace Parkway	171.775

Tombigbee	171.425
Vicksville Miltary Park	166.3, 166.9
Highway patrol	42.12, 42.18, 42.16, 42.24, 42.08, 42.3, 45.22, 42.02, 45.02

Cities: Emergency Services

Biloxi	154.89, 154.385, 155.4
Columbus	460.45, 154.43, 462.95
Gulfport	155.37, 154.13, 155.49
Hattiesburg	Trunked 856-861, 154.445, 45.18, 45.1, 45.3, 155.1
Meridian	460.125, 453.8, 155.385

MISSOURI

Forestry/Conservation	151.325, 151.415, 151.22, 151.475, 151.4, 151.265, 151.355
Fish/Game	151.19, 151.16, 151.37

Recreation, Tourism, Parks, Forests, and Monuments

Anheiser Busch	153.32, 153.125
Arrowhead Stadium	464.775
Big Surf Water Park	154.57
Broken Arrow Marina	461.125
Busch Stadium	464.675, 464.375
Fantastic Caverns	463.4125
Forest Park Art Muse	461.5875
GeoWashCarver Mon	168.35
Jefferson Memorial	154.57
KC Chiefs	464.325, 464.775
Mark Twain Nat'l Forest	168.05, 168.075, 168.1
Ozark National Riverways	171.625, 172.475
Ozark Scenic Tours	157.62, 157.68
Silver Dollar City	151.685, 151.835, 152.3
Six Flags	464.325, 464.3875
St Louis Zoo	155.805

Vacation World	464.875
Wilson's Creek Battle	173.7625
Worlds of Fun	463.425
Highway patrol	42.06, 42.22, 42.12, 42.32,
	154.905, 154.92, 460.1875,
	155.895, 155.37

Cities: Emergency Services

Columbia	155.31, 154.19, 155.145
Jefferson City	156.21, 154.4, 154.86
Joplin	Trunked 856-861, 154.875,
	154.43, 155.7
Kansas City	Trunked 856-861, 154.86,
	154.13, 462.95, 154.74
St. Joseph	Trunked 856-861, 460.15,
	460.6, 460.225, 460.625
St. Louis	Trunked 856-861

MONTANA

Forestry/Conservation	151.175, 151.19, 151.22,
	151.25, 151.37, 151.475,
	31.14, 31.26
Fish/Game	155.925, 155.07, 155.13,
	155.505, 155.565, 39.82, 39.56

Recreation, Tourism, Parks, Forests, and Monuments

Beaverhead National Forest	171.425
Beef Trail Ski	155.16, 155.22
Big Horn Canyon	166.3
Big Horn Cty Fair	33.4
Bitterroot National Forest	168.75
Custer Battlefield	167.15
Custer National For	171.0
Discovery Basin Ski	151.685
Flathead National Forest	164.375

Gallatin National Forest	164.825, 166.375
Glacier National Park	166.975, 164.375, 163.075
Grant-Kohrs Historic Site	168.35
Great Falls Ski	155.16
Helena National Forest	169.95
Kootenai National Forest	171.2625, 172.075
Lewis & Clark Nat'l Forest	168.775
Lolo National Forest	164.7, 164.9125
Winter Fair	463.3
Yellowstone National Park	166.375
Highway patrol	154.92, 154.68, 154.665, 154.785, 154.815, 155.445, 155.79, 153.905

Cities: Emergency Services

Billings	156.61, 154.37, 155.67
Boseman	155.67, 154.25, 155.325
Helena	154.755, 154.445, 155.325
Missoula	155.61, 154.145, 155.28

NEBRASKA

Forestry/Conservation	151.475, 164.125, 168.625, 169.650
Fish/Game	159.33, 151.205

Recreation, Tourism, Parks, Forests, and Monuments

Boys Town	463.875
Cornhusker Raceway	151.955
Doorly Zoo	464.4
Homestead Nat'l Monument	169.65
Nebraska National Forest	164.125, 168.625
Peony Park	464.2
Porsche Club	151.925
Scotts Bluff Nat'l Monument	417.575
State patrol	42.46, 42.3, 42.04, 42.2, 42.34, 465.525, 39.9

Cities: Emergency Services

Lincoln   Trunked 856-861, 855.9875,
                           155.22
Omaha   460.1, 154.19, 462.975
Scotts Bluff   Trunked 856-865, 154.95,
                           154.445, 39.82

NEVADA

Forestry/Conservation   158.895, 159.345, 159.27,
                               151.175, 151.25, 151.295,
                               151.19, 151.22, 151.325
Fish/Game   151.475, 151.475, 151.46
Recreation, Tourism, Parks,
Forests, and Monuments
Boulder Dam   164.475
Consumer Elec Show   153.935, 464.825, 451.225
Humboldt National Forest   169.9, 171.475
Lake Mead Rec Area   166.3, 168.35, 156.8
Las Vegas Downs   461.175
Las Vegas Speedway   463.3
Modoc National Forest   168.75, 169.125, 169.95
Nissan 400   151.625, 464.55
Tahoe National Forest   168.175, 168.775, 171.5
Toiyabe National Forest   169.875, 411.325
Wet 'n Wild   464.375, 466.3
Highway patrol   42.94, 42.78, 42.56, 42.88,
                               42.7, 42.5, 42.58, 154.695,
                               154.92, 154.905, 154.755,
                               154.665

Cities: Emergency Services

Carson City   155.97, 154.43, 155.175
Las Vegas   158.97, 159.09, 158.745,
                               159.15, 453.15, 453.1,
                               159.21, 156.21, 122.95

| Laughlin | 158.85, 154.34, 156.21 |
| Reno | 453.65, 453.7, 453.75 |

Las Vegas Entertainment

Casinos/Hotels

Aladdin	Trunked 856-859
Bally's	462.825, 460.8875, 463.7875
Barbary Coast	464.225, 464.75, 851.785
Boardwalk	154.57, 464.325
Caesar's Palace	451.7, 463.4, 461.775
California	461.05, 854.3875
Circus Circus	451.575, 464.375, 463.575
Continental	151.925, 464.375, 464.2
Desert Inn	463.575, 464.425
El Cortez	464.2625
Excalibur	853.4875, 855.2875
Flamingo Hilton	151.655, 151.685
Frontier	151.745, 855.5625
Golden Nugget	Trunked 861—866
Hacienda	154.6, 463.475, 464.725
Las Vegas Hilton	451.225, 451.475
Luxor	Trunked 856—861
Maxim	464.850, 858.8375
Mirage	852.6375
Nevada Palace	464.175
Riviera	463.875, 464.4, 463.6
Sahara	464.525
Sands	462.050, 460.912
Showboat	461.425
Stardust	464.2, 464.575, 464.725
Tropicana	855.5875, 929.0625
Whiskey Pete's	461.525, 462.175, 463.2

NEW HAMPSHIRE

Forestry/Conservation	151.445, 151.295, 159.225, 856.2125, 171.525, 173.7625
Fish/Game	151.340, 159.465, 151.325
Recreation, Tourism, Parks, Forests, and Monuments	
Appalachia Mtn Club	33.04, 461.5
Black Mtn Tramways	154.515
Canobie Lake Park	154.57, 154.6, 154.625
Conway Scenic RR	161.25
Jackson Ski Tours	152.3
NH Int'l Speedway	151.625, 154.57
Pine Acres Recreation	151.655, 154.57
Randolph Mtn Club	462.575
St. Gaudens Hist Site	173.7625
USA Speedway	154.57
White Mtn National Forest	171.525
Wilderness Plantation	464.3125
State police	44.94, 44.82, 45.26, 45.3, 45.22, 45.46, 45.18, 45.02, 44.86, 156.09, 155.91
Cities: Emergency Services	
Concord	155.625, 154.355, 155.385
Manchester	156.21, 460.625, 154.965
Nashua	460.1, 154.325, 155.175

NEW JERSEY

Forestry/Conservation	151.415, 151.475, 151.265, 159.375, 159.465, 151.415, 151.475, 151.265
Fish/Game	151.19, 159.3, 151.325, 159.345, 159.465, 159.375

Recreation, Tourism, Parks, Forests, and Monuments

Atlantic City Raceway	154.57, 464.525
Convention Center	453.35, 453.675
Edison National Hist Site	164.475, 164.4375
Five Mile Beach	44.54
Flemington Speedway	151.625
Great America	151.715, 154.6
Hidden Valley Ski	154.54, 155.22, 155.34
Monmouth Park	154.515, 154.57, 464.825
Morristown Hist Park	164.475
Outdoor World Lake	151.655
Ripcord Paracenter	151.925
Six Flags	154.54, 462.725, 464.675
Wall Stadium	154.57
State Police	44.78, 45.0, 460.5, 460.475, 155.46, 154.92, 154.935, 154.905, 156.12, 154.68, 154.725, 153.785
Remainder trunked	856-861MHz

Cities: Emergency Services

Atlantic City	460.425, 154.025, 155.22, 460.15, 453.35, 155.13
Jersey City	460.025, 460.55, 460.05
Newark	460.125, 460.15, 154.13, 155.4, 155.34, 868.8125
Trenton	453.375, 460.575, 155.265

Atlantic City Entertainment

Casinos/Hotels

Bally's Grand	461.6125, 464.125, 464.175
Bally's Park Place	463.6, 464.1, 464.575
Caesar's Palace	461.8625, 461.925, 461.95
Harrah's Marina	154.6, 462.1625, 463.75
Resorts International	154.57, 461.1125, 464.675
The Sands	463.325, 463.5, 462.0
Trump Castle	463.2, 463.35, 464.475
Trump Plaza	461.5125, 463.35, 461.825
Trump Taj Mahal	460.8, 469.3375, 854.7875

NEW MEXICO

Forestry/Conservation	159.42, 159.225, 159.33, 158.805
Fish/Game	44.8, 44.92

Recreation, Tourism, Parks, Forests, and Monuments

Angel Fire Ski Resort	463.325, 463.625
Aztec National Monument	166.35
Bandelier Nat'l Monument	164.425
Carlsbad Caverns	164.425
Carson National Forest	169.175
Chaco Culture Park	166.35
Cibola National Forest	171.45, 170.425, 172.225
El Malpais National Monu	168.275
El Morro National Monu	166.35, 166.95
Gila National Forest	169.175, 169.975
Lincoln National Forest	168.6, 168.625, 170.5
NM Desert Racing	462.05
Pecos National Monument	164.425
Rio Costilla	461.3
Rio Grande Nat'l Forest	164.15, 164.9875
Roadrunner Camp	461.525, 463.225, 154.54
Santa Fe Downs	464.425, 464.4625
Santa Fe National Forest	172.3
Seven Flags Raceway	154.6
White Sands Nat'l Monument	166.375
State Police	155.37, 155.55, 154.92, 154.8, 155.475, 155.43, 460.15, 37.06, 155.52, 155.535, 155.565, 155.655, 155.58, 155.685, 155.79, 155.73

Cities: Emergency Services

Albuquerque	Trunked 856-861, 155.85, 155.49, 154.4, 460.625

Las Cruces	Trunked 856-861, 155.19, 154.4, 154.815
Roswell	10011101001 at 124.52 GHz
Santa Fe	Trunked 856-861, 851.3875, 154.31, 154.65, 154.785

NEW YORK

Forestry/Conservation	151.22, 151.28, 151.25, 151.265, 159.225, 159.33, 159.465
Fish/Game	166.325, 167.075, 168.55
Recreation, Tourism, Parks, Forests, and Monuments	
Adirondack Ski	154.515, 155.22
Allegheny State Park	155.7
Alpine Rec Area	462.1625
Baseball Hall of Fame	461.075, 461.5, 464.825
Belmont Park	151.685, 151.835
Buffalo Bills	154.6, 467.0, 467.85
Catskill Ski	151.715
Chenango Valley	31.26
Edison National Hist Site	164.475
Ellis Island	166.325, 417.925
Erie Cty Fairgrounds	154.57
FDR Historic Site	166.95
Finger Lakes St Park	44.72
Fire Island	166.9
Gateway Rec Area	166.325, 167.075, 166.875
Genesee Cty Museum	151.895
Grant National Memorial	171.05
Holland Speedway	151.28, 151.625, 152.3
Islanders	467.9
Islip Speedway	35.18
Jets	151.625, 151.835
Lake George	154.54

Lake Otsego	151.775
Lancaster Speedway	151.625, 151.955
Lebanon Val Speedway	151.625
Long Island St Park	151.325
Mets	151.625, 151.835
Midstate Raceway	464.2
Mystic Mtn Ski	155.175, 155.22, 155.34
Niagara Falls	155.685
Niagara Falls	461.3
Oriskany Battlefield	151.145
Palisades Interstate Pk	154.89
Rangers	467.875
Raritan Arsenal	166.95
Riverhead Raceway	464.5, 464.9
Rochester War Memorial	453.5
Roosevelt Raceway	462.625, 42.96
Saratoga National Park	173.7625
Saratoga Racetrack	464.975
Saratoga Springs	155.43
Ski Valley	155.205, 155.22
Statue of Liberty	166.325, 34.79, 417.85
Thousand Islands	151.4
Ultralight Aviation	151.895
Vanderbilt Mansion	166.95
Watkins Glen	151.295, 155.34, 464.775
West Point	155.265
Windham Mtn Ski	154.54
Yankees	151.625
State Police	155.505, 154.905, 155.655, 155.445, 155.46, 155.595, 154.95, 154.74, 154.68, 155.52, 154.665

Cities: Emergency Services

Albany	Trunked 856-861, 154.415, 155.22, 460.4
Buffalo	460.425, 154.19, 460.475
Cooperstown	155.73, 46.44, 155.235

New York City

Citywide fire	154.43
Manhattan	476.5625, 476.3375, 476.5875, 476.3125, 476.3625, 476.6375
Bronx	477.0625, 476.9625 476.9125, 476.6625
Brooklyn	476.4625, 476.4125, 477.0875, 476.8625, 476.9875, 477.1375
Queens	477.1125, 477.0125, 476.9375, 476.4875
Staten Island	476.6125, 476.3875
Niagara Falls	460.375, 460.575, 154.755
Rochester	460.025, 154.31, 155.175
Syracuse	460.475, 153.95, 155.265

New York City Entertainment

Apollo Theater	461.7625, 461.7875
Battery Park	154.57
Bronx Zoo	154.57
Brooklyn Museum	154.6, 453.55, 453.575
Central Park Conserv	463.5125
Cooper-Hewitt Museum	33.4
Empire State Bldg	463.45
Guggenheim Museum	154.57
Intrepid Museum	463.925
Jewish Museum	461.0625
Lincoln Center	464.925
Madison Square Garden	154.6, 154.514, 154.57
Metropolitan Museum	154.57, 464.425
Metropolitan Opera	151.835, 154.54, 157.74
Museum Modern Art	157.74
Museum of History	151.805
NY Aquarium	469.875
NY Stock Exchange	462.1, 464.0875, 464.35
Radio City Music Hall	464.675, 464.775, 464.925
Rockefeller Center	154.54, 463.2875, 463.4375

Roosevelt Island	464.15, 461.0125
Staten Island Ferry	156.95, 158.73
Whitney Museum	154.57, 154.6
YMCA	154.6, 464.3125

NORTH CAROLINA

Forestry/Conservation   31.34, 31.42, 31.46, 31.54, 30.98, 31.22, 31.26, 151.175, 159.39

Fish/Game   159.315, 159.345, 159.285, 159.225, 151.22, 151.325, 151.385

Recreation, Tourism, Parks, Forests, and Monuments

Appalachia Ski Mtn	154.54
Awanquarter Refuge	34.83
Beech Mtn Ski	461.625, 463.475, 155.16
Billy Graham Assn	461.95, 463.8, 463.875
Blue Ridge Parkway	166.375, 167.175
Cape Hatteras	164.2, 164.725, 169.65
Cape Lookout	169.65
Carl Sandberg Site	171.675, 171.775
Charlotte Coliseum	453.75, 463.8625, 463.7625
Charlotte Speedway	151.835, 151.895, 462.55
Cherokee National Forest	168.675
Chimney Rock Park	154.54
Croatan National Forest	168.725
Crystal Beach	154.57
Dixieland Speedway	464.325, 464.575
Great Smokie Mountains	166.35, 167.15
Kisatchie National Forest	169.925
Lake Gaston	151.655
Nantahala National Forest	171.475
NC Motor Speedway	464.7, 469.9375
NC Museum Life/Sci	464.875

NC Museum of Art	155.94
Pea Island Refuge	34.83
Pisgah National Forest	168.725, 171.475
Uwharrie National Forest	168.725
Highway Patrol	42.62, 42.52, 42.78, 42.8, 42.6, 42.66, 42.64, 42.76, 42.5, 42.7, 42.82, 155.445

Cities: Emergency Services

Charlotte	Trunked 851-861
Durham	453.3, 453.9, 453.5
Fayetteville	460.3, 460.625, 155.28
Greensboro	460.1, 154.445, 460.325
Raleigh	460.15, 154.37, 155.205
Wilmington	453.4, 154.13, 155.28

NORTH DAKOTA

Forestry/Conservation and Fish/Game	151.175, 151.43, 151.415, 151.34, 151.445

Recreation, Tourism, Parks, Forests, and Monuments

Dacotah Speedway	460.8875
Ft. Union Monument	166.375
Knife River Indian Vil	166.375
Nodak Race Club	464.825
Skyriders Ultralights	154.57
Teddy Roosevelt Park	166.375
Highway Patrol	154.905, 154.935, 155.43, 155.505, 155.475, 155.37, 156.03, 453.45

Cities: Emergency Servicess

Bismarck	155.07, 453.3, 154.65
Fargo	453.5, 453.2, 155.265
Moorhead	155.085, 154.1, 155.265

OHIO

Forestry/Conservation	151.34, 151.415, 151.445, 151.43
Fish/Game	151.355, 154.935

Recreation, Tourism, Parks, Forests, and Monuments

Bengals	460.275, 461.75, 462.175
Cincinatti Coliseum	469.975
Cincinatti Museum	463.425, 463.8
Cleveland Stadium	154.57, 154.6
Cuyahoga Valley Area	166.375
Dayton Air Show	122.775, 461.0875, 461.4625
Indians	154.515
Irish Cultural Festival	151.625
King's Island	154.54, 463.675, 464.775
Mound City Monument	166.375
Ohio State Fair	151.625, 151.025, 151.715
Perry's Victory Memorial	170.1
Reds	460.275, 461.75, 462.175
Sea World of Ohio	154.54, 154.6, 462.025
Wayne National Forest	164.825
Highway Patrol	44.94, 45.26, 44.98, 44.82, 44.74, 44.86, 465.55, 465.375, 465.425, 465.525, 154.935
Radar, aircraft	45.02

Cities: Emergency Services

Akron	Trunked 851-857, 460.375, 460.5, 460.6, 462.95
Cincinnati	Trunked 866-869, 460.2, 460.6, 460.275, 460.525
Cleveland	Trunked 851-856, 33.9, 155.16, 460.15, 460.275
Columbus	Trunked 856-861, 154.31, 154.4, 155.34, 460.1

Dayton	Trunked 856-861, 155.415, 155.67
Toledo	Trunked 851-856, 460.475, 154.19, 462.95, 192.8

OKLAHOMA

Forestry/Conservation	159.39, 158.76, 159.45, 159.225, 151.235, 151.25, 151.28, 151.31, 151.37
Fish/Game	44.64, 44.84, 44.96, 156.015, 155.49

Recreation, Tourism, Parks, Forests, and Monuments

Chickasaw Rec Area	168.425
Cibola National Forest	170.425
Oklahoma City Zoo	153.815
Oklahoma State Fair	154.54, 460.825, 464.025
Ouachita National Forest	169.175, 169.675
Tulsa Assembly Ctr	453.975
Highway Patrol	42.7, 44.9, 45.22, 45.18, 154.905, 465.5625
Aircraft	138.05
Remainder trunked	856-866 MHz

Cities: Emergency Services

Lawton	453.25, 453.4, 453.35
Muskogee	460.1, 460.35, 154.43
Oklahoma City	158.79, 159.09, 159.03, 453.35, 462.95, 158.97
Tulsa	Trunked 856-861, 453.05, 153.755, 155.07, 158.91

OREGON

Forestry/Conservation169.875, 170.5, 164.1,
                                    164.7, 169.925, 169.95,
                                    168.625, 170.1
Fish/Game   151.145, 151.16, 151.175,
                                    151.19, 151.205, 151.22,
                                    151.34, 155.805, 47.16

Recreation, Tourism, Parks,
Forests, and Monuments
Clark County Fair   461.0875
Crater Lake National Park   170.1, 169.55, 168.625
Deschutes National Forest   169.875, 170.475, 170.5
Freemont National Forest   171.7, 172.35
Hells Canyon Nat'l Forest   164.1, 164.7
High Desert Museum   461.0125, 461.0375
Hunter Expeditions   461.45
John Day Fossil Beds   169.725
Medford Speedway   154.54
Mission Hill Museum   464.675, 464.875
Mt Hood Mdws Ski   151.835
Mt Hood National Forest   169.925, 169.95, 170.5
Ochoco National Forest   169.175, 169.975, 170.5
OR Coast Aquarium   461.225, 464.975
OR Country Fair   464.525, 464.875
Oregon Caves   164.425, 171.625
Portland Coliseum   453.35, 462.575, 462.7625
Portland Int'l Speedway   461.0875, 461.5375
Rogue River National For   168.625, 169.175, 169.975
Siskiyou National Forest   170.5, 171.15
Summit Ski   463.25
Valley River Center   461.050, 461.575
Wallowa-Whitman   164.15, 164.8, 164.825
Wash Cty Fairground   462.8375, 464.7875
Wash Park Zoo   151.655, 462.1

Willamette National Forest	164.825, 164.9125
Willamette Pass Ski	463.4
State Police	42.88, 42.94, 42.82, 42.86, 42.56, 42.9, 42.92, 42.86, 154.935, 154.86, 154.905, 154.695, 155.475

Cities: Emergency Services

Bend	Trunked 856-861
Eugene	460.3, 155.16, 154.355
Medford	156.57, 154.16, 156.09
Portland	Trunked 855-861, 460.325, 460.2, 154.01, 462.95

PENNSYLVANIA

Forestry/Conservation	151.16, 151.175, 151.295, 151.385, 151.4
Fish/Game	44.64, 44.84, 44.88, 45.04, 44.96, 44.84, 44.7, 45.3

Recreation, Tourism, Parks, Forests, and Monuments

Allegheny National Forest	171.525
Big Boulder Ski	155.235
Big Diamond Racing	464.925
Blue Knob Rec Area	154.54
Delaware Watergap	166.95
Dorney Park Coaster	151.655, 154.57
Eagles	151.775
Flyers	49.83, 49.875
Fort Necessity	172.4
Gettysburg	164.725
Grandview Speedway	469.875
Hershey Park	464.15, 464.975
Idlewild Park	151.865
Independence Park	164.725

Nazareth Fairgrounds	151.835
Nazareth Raceway	154.57
PA Int'l Speedway	151.625
Phillies	154.57, 151.775, 464.95
Pirates	151.625
Shawnee Mtn Ski	464.875
Strasburg Hist Site	453.725
Tanglewood Ski	154.515, 152.22
Three River Stadium	467.85, 467.925, 467.75
Towanda	162.475
Valley Forge	164.425
Washington Crossing	153.935
Wellsboro	162.55
Whitewater Challenge	461.9
Wilkes-Barre	162.55
State Police	155.58, 155.79, 154.95, 155.67, 155.91, 155.505, 155.85, 154.755, 154.475, 42.6, 159.0, 159.045

Cities: Emergency Services

Allentown	158.79, 453.475, 159.09
Harrisburg	460.275, 453.7, 460.3
Philadelphia	Trunked 866-869, 453.05, 453.25, 453.3, 153.95
Pittsburgh	Trunked 856-861, 453.1, 453.25, 453.4, 462.95

Philadelphia tourism

Civic Center	460.45
Convention Center	464.5
Eagle Bounds Racing	407.8875
Franklin Mint	451.475, 462.425
Liberty Bell Park	151.685
Smithville Hist Town	463.525
Veterans Stadium	154.57, 154.6, 464.95
Zoo	151.655, 151.685, 154.57

RHODE ISLAND

Forestry/Conservation	31.54, 31.58, 31.62, 31.74,
and Fish/Game	151.175, 151.385, 158.97, 154.28

Recreation, Tourism, Parks,
Forests, and Monuments

Atlantic Beach Park	151.805
Blackstone Valley	151.955
Rocky Pt Amus Park	154.57, 464.775, 464.825
Roger Williams Zoo	464.925
Prov Perf Arts Ctr	464.325, 464.45
Special Olympics	464.575, 464.875
Tuna Tournament	151.745, 462.6
State Police	155.505, 155.61, 154.935,
	154.905, 155.445, 155.19, 158.97
Radar	155.475

Cities: Emergency Services

Jamestown	155.07, 153.95
Newport	155.73, 155.685, 154.22
Providence	460.1, 154.37, 460.425

SOUTH CAROLINA

Forestry/Conservation	159.27, 159.3, 159.345,
	159.405, 159.45, 151.19,
	151.265, 164.925, 31.78
Fish/Game	151.445, 151.43, 151.295,
	151.16, 151.415, 151.250

Recreation, Tourism, Parks,
Forests, and Monuments

Baker Creek	453.325
Barnwell	453.5
Billy Dreher Island	453.325, 453.5

Carolina Coastal Fair	151.835
Charleston Air Fair	464.95
Charleston Museum	464.35
Cheraw	453.775
Congaree Swamp	169.775
Cowpens Battlefield	171.775
Croft	453.875
Edisto Beach	453.475
Frances Marion Forest	168.675, 168.075
Ft. Moultrie	170.05
Ft. Sumter	170.05
Hamilton Branch	453.325
Harris Mountain	453.875
Hickory Knob Resort	453.325
Hunting Island	453.725
Huntington Beach	453.925
International Speedway	463.4375, 464.775
King's Mountain	171.775, 453.775
Lake Greenwood	453.5
Lake Hartwell	453.325
Lake Wateree	453.475
Little Pee Dee	453.925
Myrtle Beach	453.925, 151.715, 461.35
National Forests Statewide	170.525
Oconee	453.325
Patriot's Pt. Museum	453.3
Point Sett	453.475
Riverbanks Zoo	453.325
Saddler's Creek	453.875
Santee	453.725
SC Peach Festival	154.57
Sesqui	453.325, 453.5
State Museum	453.55
Sumter National Forest	168.675
Table Rock	453.875
Highway Patrol	42.1, 42.26, 42.12, 42.08,
	42.34, 42.14, 42.06,

155.955, 155.445, 460.25,
460.05, 460.275, 453.45

Cities: Emergency Services

Charleston	Trunked 856-861, 158.73, 158.85, 460.6, 155.07
Columbia	Trunked 851-861, 460.125, 460.025, 453.1, 155.22
Greenville	460.075, 460.1, 453.9
Spartanburg	460.225, 460.25, 154.07

SOUTH DAKOTA

Forestry/Conservation	151.145, 151.28, 151.355, 151.385, 151.4, 151.445
Fish/Game	39.18

Recreation, Tourism, Parks, Forests, and Monuments

Badlands National Park	169.4, 170.05, 169.95
Black Hills National Forest	166.575, 169.6, 170.55
Black Hills Speedway	464.3
Buffalo Gap	164.125
Custer National Forest	169.175
Hills Convention Ctr.	151.685
Jewell Cave	170.05
Medicine Bow	164.15, 164.95
Mt. Rushmore	170.05, 169.4
Nebraska National Forest	164.125
S. Dakota Gaming	461.825
Sioux Empire Fair	461.6
State Fair	464.975
Wildlife Research Ltd	151.955
Wind Cave National Park	170.05, 169.4
Highway Patrol	39.1, 39.12, 39.32, 39.24, 39.28, 39.16, 39.36, 453.375

Cities: Emergency Services
Pierre   453.9, 453.3, 154.25
Rapid City   453.9, 453.1, 460.575
Sioux Falls   460.125, 155.88, 463.825

TENNESSEE

Forestry/Conservation   159.405, 159.45, 151.16,
                            453.45, 453.25, 453.2,
                            464.675, 151.445
Fish/Game   159.3, 159.24, 151.235,
                            159.465, 151.415

**Recreation, Tourism, Parks,
Forests, and Monuments**
Barbara Mandrell   154.6
Big South Fork   163.075, 170.575
Blue Ridge Parkway   167.175
Chattanooga Conv Ctr   461.85
Chattanooga Mil Park   168.325
Cherokee National Forest 168.075, 168.675, 169.875
Chickamauga Park   168.325
Chickasau Park   453.45
Cumberland Gap   166.7875, 166.3
Cumberland Mtn   151.16
Dollywood   463.7, 463.825, 463.925
Elvis Presley Enterpri   151.655, 151.925
Frozen Head Park   151.16
Ft. Donelson   167.15
Great Smoky Mtns   167.15, 167.075, 166.35
Hiawassee Park   151.16
Jack Daniels Tours   152.42, 464.2, 464.825
Johnny Walker Tours   462.05
Kingsport Speedway   154.54, 464.3375
Libertyland   464.775, 464.825
Mid South Fair   464.675, 464.975

Nashville Speedway	151.955
Nature Center	151.655
Oakridge Boys	464.225
Obed River	163.075
Opryland USA	156.9, 464.25, 464.8
Orpheum Theatre	466.8625, 466.9625
Panther Creek	151.16
Pickwick Park	453.25
Roan Mountain	151.16
Shiloh National Mil Park	164.425
Silver Dollar City	464.675, 464.7
Stones River Cemetar	172.775
Tim's Ford Park	453.2
TN Aquarium	461.45, 461.675, 461.875
TN State Fair	464.675
Highway Patrol	42.42, 42.26, 42.56, 42.36, 45.58, 45.62, 45.66, 45.7, 42.28, 154.905, 159.09, 158.73, 154.86, 154.77, 158.835, 155.025

Cities: Emergency Services

Chattanooga	Trunked 856-861, 460.075, 154.22, 460.125, 460.275
Jackson	Trunked 856-861, 460.025, 460.5, 154.445, 155.205
Knoxville	Trunked 856-861
Memphis	Trunked 856-861, 460.35, 460.025, 460.175, 460.25
Nashville	155.01, 155.13, 155.07, 155.31, 154.86, 460.575, 155.535, 463.025, 462.95

TEXAS

Forestry/Conservation	159.225, 159.36, 159.375, 159.33, 159.465, 164.825, 171.475, 170.425, 170.575
Fish/Game	159.27, 151.415, 151.355, 151.34, 151.31, 159.345, 151.490, 159.36

Recreation, Tourism, Parks, Forests, and Monuments

Amistad Rec Area	166.325
Angelina	171.475, 171.575, 170.575
Big Bend National Park	166.375
Big Thicket	166.9
Caddo Grassland	171.475
Chamizal Memorial	164.425
Cibola	170.425, 171.45, 172.35
Davey Crockett	170.575, 168.75, 169.95
Ft. Davis	164.425
Joe Freeman Coliseu	463.9625, 464.1125, 464.375
Lake Crockett	171.475
Lake Meredith	166.9
LBJ Grassland	171.475
LBJ Historical Park	170.075
Natural Bridge	30.76
Padre Island Seashore	166.9
Rio Grande	163.125
Riverplace	464.575
Sabine	170.575, 168.75, 169.95
Sam Houston	171.475, 171.575, 168.75
Sea World	464.575, 464.1875
State Aquarium	461.85, 463.525, 464.725
Wonderland Park	154.57
World Speedway	154.54
Highway Patrol	154.68, 155.46, 154.95,

155.37, 155.505, 158.73,
155.445, 154.695, 159.09,
159.15, 159.21, 154.665

Cities: Emergency Services

Abilene	154.785, 154.445, 155.28
Amarillo	153.89, 154.86, 462.95
Austin	460.4, 453.45, 460.45
Corpus Christi	Trunked 856-861, 154.19, 154.385, 154.95, 154.785
Dallas	Trunked 856-869, 460.325, 460.375, 460.425, 154.415
Fort Worth	Trunked 866-868, 856.4375
Houston	460.1, 460.425, 460.225, 453.425, 462.95, 460.325
San Antonio	Trunked 856-861
Waco	Trunked 856-861, 154.875, 460.55, 154.28, 155.73

UTAH

Forestry/Conservation	151.235, 151.415, 151.37, 151.28, 151.145, 155.16, 171.475, 170.0, 168.625
Fish/Game	151.265, 155.775, 155.265

Recreation, Tourism, Parks, Forests, and Monuments

Alta Ski	154.515, 453.0375
Ashley National Forest	171.475, 170.0
Beaver Mtn Ski	464.6
Bonneville Speedway	151.685
Brian Head Ski	461.65, 461.95
Bryce Canyon	172.5, 168.575
Canyonlands	166.325, 166.925
Capitol Reef	168.575
Cedar Breaks	166.325

Dinosaur Nat'l Monument	166.375
Dixie National Forest	168.625, 171.55
Fishlake	169.175, 169.975
Glen Canyon	171.625, 171.675, 156.425
Golden Spike	171.675
Natural Bridges	166.925
Salt Lake Civic Auditorium	158.82
Snowbird Ski	154.57
Timpanogos Cave	166.15
Uinta	171.525, 171.575
Wasatch	164.975
Zion National Park	166.325
Highway Patrol	155.505, 155.745, 155.595, 155.655, 155.31, 155.91, 155.685, 155.58, 155.625, 155.61, 155.65, 465.125, 465.175

Cities: Emergency Services

Brigham City	
Ogden	460.5, 154.25, 460.25
Provo	155.19, 154.07, 154.19
Salt Lake City	Trunked 856-861, 460.1, 460.15, 155.205, 154.43, 460.375, 460.3, 460.2
LDS (Mormon) Corporation	151.835, 461.0625, 461.325, 461.55, 461.7375, 462.5, 464.3875, 463.775, 463.925, 464.0, 464.225, 464.45, 466.4625, 461.525, 463.5125

VERMONT

Forestry/Conservation	151.475, 169.175
Fish/Game	159.405

Recreation, Tourism, Parks, Forests, and Monuments

Bolton Valley Ski	151.655
Brattleboro Retreat	157.56
Green Mtn National Forest	169.175
Green Mtn Racetrack	154.6
Mount Snow Ski	171.745, 461.35
Mountaintop Ski	151.625, 151.715
Mt. Nordic Ski	152.3
Pico Peak Ski	154.54, 151.685
Rossignol Ski Co.	462.225, 151.895
Shellburne Museum	151.895
Sugarbush Resort	151.805, 152.3, 151.995
State Police	460.225, 460.15, 460.375, 460.425, 460.475, 458.95, 460.5, 460.025, 460.275

Cities: Emergency Services

Burlington	460.125, 460.625, 460.5
Montpelier	460.05, 460.5, 154.01
Rutland	460.375, 460.2, 460.525

VIRGINIA

Forestry/Conservation	151.235, 151.4, 39.5, 39.54, 170.05, 411.7, 168.425, 166.3, 166.95, 166.9
Fish/Game	151.28, 151.43, 159.435

Recreation, Tourism, Parks, Forests, and Monuments

Appomattox Historic Site	166.35
Assateague Seashore	170.05
B. T. Washington	411.7, 166.35
Blue Ridge Parkway	167.175
Busch Gardens	463.425, 463.775, 463.575
Chrysler Museum	154.57, 154.6

Colonial Historic Park	167.15, 168.425
Colonial Williamsburg	463.625, 463.3375, 151.775
Cumberland Gap Park	166.3, 166.7875
Fredericksburg Mil Pk	166.95
Geo Wash Birthplace	163.125
Geo Wash Mem Pkw	169.775, 172.75
Geo Wash National Forest	171.425, 171.525
Harper's Ferry	168.425
Jefferson Memorial	464.375
Jefferson National Forest	171.575
Langley Speedway	154.57, 154.6
Manassas Battlefield	163.125
Mariner's Museum	151.835
Martinsville Speedway	154.54
National Convention Ctr	151.955
Petersburg Battlefield	164.475
Prince William Forest	170.05
Richmond Raceway	464.55
Shenandoah National Park	166.9
Spotsylvania Battlefld	166.95
Virginia Beach	155.295
State Police	159.0, 154.935, 158.985, 154.905, 159.165, 155.445, 159.135, 155.46, 154.695, 154.665, 453.35, 458.35, 39.5

Cities: Emergency Services

Chesapeake	155.13, 154.415, 155.73
Newport News	453.65, 154.13, 453.6
Norfolk	Trunked 852-861, 462.975, 156.21
Portsmouth	Trunked 856-861, 453.2, 39.56
Richmond	460.1, 453.75, 460.325
Roanoke	Trunked 854-861, 155.13, 155.49, 154.31

WASHINGTON

Forestry/Conservation	151.415, 159.42, 159.36, 159.255, 159.24, 159.3, 159.45, 159.375
Fish/Game	155.97, 155.37, 151.28, 159.42

Recreation, Tourism, Parks, Forests, and Monuments

Chewelah Basin Ski	151.655
Colville National Forest	168.625, 170.125, 170.425
Coulee Dam	166.375 (report all leaks)
Crystal Mountain Ski	154.515, 155.265
Ft. Vancouver	408.575
Gifford Pinchot	168.15, 168.75, 170.125
Granite Point Park	154.54
Hell's Canyon	164.1, 164.7
Hillbilly Fiddlers	462.55 or thereabouts
Hurricane Ridge	154.515, 154.54
Mt. Baker	168.625, 169.9, 169.925
Mt. Baker Ski	151.805
Mt. Rainier	163.2375, 163.39, 170.775
Mt. St. Helens	172.225
Museum Hist/Industry	463.7375
Museum of Flight	462.0875
North Cascades	166.75
Okanogan	165.975, 168.625, 169.875
Olympic Ski	164.125, 164.8, 164.825
Olympic National Park	168.525, 411.625
Pacific Science Ctr	461.3375
Port Angeles Speedw	49.83
San Juan Island	40.75
Ski Acres	151.715, 155.205
Snoqualmie	168.625, 169.9, 169.925
Umatilla	164.125, 164.15, 164.825
Washington Conv Ctr	461.0875, 461.1375

Washington Fair	151.925, 154.57
Wenatchee	171.5, 172.25, 413.9
State Patrol	155.97, 154.77, 155.58,
	155.52, 154.845, 154.68,
	155.85, 154.665, 154.695,
	154.935, 155.505, 154.92,
	154.755, 453.475
Aircraft	159.075

Cities: Emergency Services

Bellingham	155.07, 453.225, 154.34
Olympia	154.875, 154.43, 155.145
Seattle	Trunked 851-869, 453.8,
	462.95, 460.475, 460.075
Spokane	159.09, 159.21, 154.43
Tacoma	460.05, 460.15, 154.13
Yakima	Trunked 856-861, 156.21,
	154.43, 154.74

WEST VIRGINIA

Forestry/Conservation	31.98, 31.7, 31.58, 31.94,
	31.62, 38.55, 38.81, 166.95
Fish/Game	159.225

Recreation, Tourism, Parks, Forests, and Monuments

Canaan Valley Ski	155.16
Capital Music Hall	151.895
Harper's Ferry	168.425
Huntington Regatta	151.805
Monongahela	38.55, 38.81
Nat'l Powerboat Association	154.54
New River Gorge	166.95
SCCA	154.57, 154.6
Shenandoah	166.9
Snowshoe Ski	154.515, 462.7, 155.175

Wheeling Downs	154.57
Whitewater Rafting	464.125, 464.2, 464.4
WV State Fair	464.475
State Police	42.1, 42.12, 42.26, 155.43, 155.505, 156.15, 39.98

Cities: Emergency Services

Charleston	159.15, 154.04, 154.385
Huntington	155.52, 154.43, 45.24
Parkersburg	155.49, 154.34, 153.98

WISCONSIN

Forestry/Conservation	159.225, 159.255, 159.33, 151.4, 159.39
Fish/Game	151.16, 171.75, 164.75, 34.83

Recreation, Tourism, Parks, Forests, and Monuments

Alpine Valley Resort	151.655, 151.805, 155.16
American Adventure	151.685
Americana Ski	464.975
Angell Speedway	154.57
Cascade Mtn Ski	464.975
Chequamegon	164.825
Columbus Speedway	154.6
Dairyland Greyhound	464.6
Dodge Cty Fairground	464.325
Experimental A/C	121.6, 172.925, 464.95
Germanfest	154.57, 154.6
Great Lakes Dragway	154.57
Green Bay Packers	151.625, 469.5, 469.55
Horizon Wildlife Ref	171.75
Kenosha Cty Fair	154.57
Madison Speedway	153.08
Milwaukee Conv Ctr	154.6, 453.15
Milwaukee Expo	154.6

Necedah Wildlife Ref	34.83
Nicolet	164.9875, 168.125
Olympia Resort	464.975
Seven Mile Fair	154.57
St Croix Riverway	164.75, 164.25, 408.6
Summit Ski	154.57
Sunburst Ski	155.16, 157.68
Waterworld	151.685
WI Int'l Raceway	151.625
WI State Fair	154.965, 453.2875, 155.61
State Patrol	154.68, 159.42, 155.445,
	159.285, 154.935, 159.45,
	154.905, 155.46, 154.92

Cities: Emergency Services

Eau Claire	154.875, 155.64, 154.31
Green Bay	Trunked 856-861, 155.13,
	154.4, 154.74
Madison	460.05, 460.575, 460.3
Milwaukee	Trunked 866-869, 460.075,
	460.225, 154.385, 462.95

WYOMING

Forestry/Conservation	151.43, 151.16, 151.295,
	168.625, 169.925, 169.6,
	164.15, 169.125, 169.875
Fish/Game	155.64, 154.875, 154.785,
	166.375, 167.5875, 164.8

**Recreation, Tourism, Parks,
Forests, and Monuments**

Ashley National Forest	171.475
Bible Camping Inc.	460.95
Big Horn	169.925
Bighorn Canyon Rec	166.3
Black Hills	169.6, 169.95, 170.55

Boot Hill	154.57
Bridger-Teton	169.125
Buffalo Bill Center	157.62
Bureau of Land Mgmt	166.725, 168.25
Devil's Tower	169.4, 170.05
Fossil Butte	169.4, 170.05, 168.575
Ft. Laramie	173.7625
Grand Teton	171.675
Jackson Hole Resort	151.925, 157.56, 152.3
Lewis & Clark Exp	157.56
Medicine Bow	164.15, 164.9125
Mountain Shadow	461.05
Shoshone	169.875
Sierra Madre Foundation	154.54
Spring Creek Resort	464.475
Targhee	169.175
Wasatch	164.975
Wyoming River Trips	463.2, 461.5
Yellowstone Aircraft	168.55, 123.05, 126.75
Yellowstone Opns	166.375, 167.5875, 164.8
Yellowstone Services	463.45, 164.6
Highway Patrol	155.445, 156.75, 154.875, 155.64, 155.58

Cities: Emergency Services

Casper	154.8, 155.7, 154.31
Cheyenne	154.8, 154.4, 155.49
Laramie	155.25, 154.815, 154.31
Sheridan	154.815, 154.445, 155.76

Recommended Reading for Those Boring Motel Evenings

Here's a short list of books that will expand your scanning horizons. Every book on the list is available from Paladin Press.

Radio Monitoring
Skip Arey

Skip has written one of the most comprehensive books on monitoring you can buy. His unique combination of technology, technique, and general lore is useful to every scannist. Terrific reviews, justly deserved. Every scannist should have this important reference book.

Scanners & Secret Frequencies
Henry Eisenson

An excellent basic to intermediate scanning book, with a lot of info on scanner technology, antennas, the law, scanner products, frequencies, and much more.

The Ultimate Scanner
Bill Cheek

When the best scanner you can buy is simply not good enough, Bill Cheek can help you take the next steps. Step by step procedures for increasing memory, accelerating the scan rate adding functionality, computer interfaces, and much more.